RAYS OF THE DAWN

RAYS OF THE DAWN

NATURAL LAWS OF THE BODY, MIND, AND SOUL

DR. THURMAN FLEET

WITH FOREWORD BY GEORGE THURMAN FLEET, JR.

SECOND EDITION

CONCEPT-THERAPY INSTITUTE
SAN ANTONIO, TEXAS

RAYS OF THE DAWN
Natural Laws of the Body, Mind, and Soul

Second Edition
with Foreword by George Thurman Fleet, Jr.

Copyright © 1948, 1976 by Dr. Thurman Fleet; 2000 by the Concept-Therapy Institute.

Second Edition, published 2000

Library of Congress Catalog Card Number: 99-74667

ISBN: 978-0-9671845-0-0

FOREWORD

Dear Reader,

Every day more and more people search for a natural way to improve their health and their lives. If you are one of them, then this book is for you.

My father first introduced this material to his chiropractic patients in pamphlet form in the 1930s. It was copyrighted and published as a book in 1948. This second edition presents a Foreword, an Introduction, and an overall new look for the contemporary reader. It also includes the original final chapter, "Natural Laws and Their Relation to Health and Disease," which had been deleted from previous editions for length considerations.

Right from the early days of his chiropractic practice on, Dr. Fleet proclaimed, "There can be no healing without teaching." The *Rays of the Dawn* was an integral part of his success in getting sick people well. He knew that the emotion of fear, and accompanying emotions of anger and worry, cause much of the sickness in our world. In a straightforward, logical style, Dr. Fleet explains how to overcome these negative energy forces and transmute them into positive, healthful energy.

Over the years, many doctors have relied on this book to aid themselves and their patients. But doctors aren't the only ones who appreciate its depth and timeless relevance. This book attracts scores of other readers. Many wellness programs include *Rays of the Dawn* in their curriculum. It can be found in substance abuse hospitals, nursing homes, and correctional institutions. Catholic nuns have used it in seminars designed to ease their transition into retirement. Educational groups who serve the senior population use it. And, of course, people from all walks of life have studied *Rays of the Dawn* individually and in Study Clubs ever since Dr. Fleet first introduced it nearly three-quarters of a century ago.

My father's dream was to see the *Rays of the Dawn* eventually incorporated into school curriculums, from kindergarten through high school, so that everyone could start life with the same tool set. Until that day comes, this book will continue serving humanity one reader at a time.

Rays of the Dawn has a remarkable history and track record of helping people. Yet its pages offer no instant, magical formula. There simply is no "quick fix." Changing your life for the better takes time, study, and application. That said, you can find in these pages the path to good health, lasting happiness, and real peace of mind—as have thousands of other readers. When its message becomes a part of every fiber of your being—body and mind and soul and spirit—you will join those whose treasured copy of *Rays of the Dawn* is underlined, notated, worn, and frayed through years of service.

You will probably recognize many of the age-old, common sense truths expressed in this book. Truth never changes. What Dr. Fleet has done here, however, is present those truths in a practical, workable manner. I hope *Rays of the Dawn* inspires you toward a better life, and equips you with the tools to build it.

My best to you.

Sincerely,

George Thurman Fleet, Jr.
President
Concept-Therapy Institute
San Antonio, Texas

PREFACE

God breathed into man's nostrils the breath of life and man became a living Soul constitutes the basic precept of this book. As a Soul, each of us is confronted in this life with many vital problems, the solutions of which are of paramount importance to achieving happiness and well-being. Events concerning the soul are taking place in the world today, and each of us is, to a great extent, the pilot of our own course.

During the past there has been much misunderstanding and confusion regarding the right way and the wrong way to live in order to be in harmony with the God within. We have had centuries of superstitious credulity and metaphysical and theological dogmatization concerning humanity's spiritual relationship with God.

The world today is in chaos. Those who have "eyes to see" and "ears to hear" can only be pained and humiliated that the world is farther from real peace, farther from a new order based on mutual understanding and justice, than it has ever been before. A titanic struggle is taking place between the two forces now competing for mastery of the world. The spirit of brotherhood is in danger of being stifled and crushed because selfish desires for aggrandizement are supplanting sound reason.

We might ask the reason for all this confusion. On every side there is a feeling of uncertainty, a feeling of distress. Everywhere people question, "What is truth, what is reliable? Where can we find some rock on which to place our feet amid all the buffeting of conflicting opinions, the doubt, skepticism and unbelief?"

This book is addressed to those in need of a workable, livable philosophy of life. The message it brings is a method by which the Will of God may be enthroned in the realization of the destiny of the human soul. Its central theme is the subordination of the human will, perfect in its freedom, to the obedience of the Natural Laws which govern the Body, Mind and Soul in accordance with the purpose and Divine Plan of the Creator.

The most advanced thought of today concedes that God is within us—or that we are within God—and that God expresses as our spiritual consciousness. We should strive with intense enthusiasm and reverence toward the development of this consciousness in order that we may have Life and have it more abundantly.

Life will be glorious and happy when we realize that the Universe is one of law and order and is governed by Natural Divine Laws. As we become aware of the laws to which we are subject and learn to harmonize with them, we automatically attune ourselves with the Divine.

The individual who cooperates with natural law always benefits. Many physical ills can be cured by correct dietary measures. Many mental disorders can be cured by right thinking. Therefore, it is only logical to assume that spiritual inharmonies may be alleviated by right acting.

The laws of Nature are assuredly good. We may regard them as dependable, since they follow discernible routes which we can know. The greatest gift to humankind is the ability, through intelligence, to discern and utilize Nature's methods.

The best definition of Natural Law seems to be: "*It is the uniform and orderly method of the omnipotent God.*" Natural Law, which pervades the physical, mental, and spiritual planes of life, is God in manifestation. The human body is a part of Nature and therefore subject to its forces and laws. Our philosophies are filled with statements asserting that we have a mind that is governed by mental laws. All our religions begin with the precept that each of us is a soul. Religions outline certain rules of conduct that the soul should abide by. Therefore, a thinking person will not dispute the fact that the body, mind, and soul are, like everything else in the universe, governed by certain laws. The question is, what are the laws?

This work offers certain rules or laws as an answer, but it does not maintain that all the laws are embodied herein. This work merely offers a set of rules that you may examine critically to determine whether or not they are beneficial.

When the human soul was created, it was given certain powers that no other form of life possessed; namely, the POWER OF CHOICE or FREE WILL. Certain responsibilities have been placed upon the soul in the exercise of this power. Our capacity to choose, therefore, does not involve freedom from the consequences of the choice.

The laws or rules which govern us, and which are outlined in this work, are as exact as the laws which govern the material universe. We may act in accordance with these laws or disregard them, but we cannot in any way alter them. The law forever operates and holds us to strict accountability. We are punished or rewarded according to the way in which we utilize the law. We may act as we choose, but we cannot escape the inevitable consequence of the act. We may have faith or fear, but we cannot avoid the reaction upon our own physical, mental, and spiritual being. Nature (or God) within always operates according to law—never by chance. With our intellect and gift of reason we may, if we desire, become allies working in harmony with law, or we may act contrary to it, but the law determines the result or consequence of that choice.

Throughout the long history of humanity's evolution, life has been a battle. We have fought among the species and among our own kind. Ignorance of the natural laws of life, which bring peace and harmony, caused a desire for power, self-assertion, exaggerated ambition and greed. Terrible suffering resulted. Our warfare against our own kind has been physical, mental and spiritual. Discord, strife and war continue still. The world today is suffering from the Will to Power, and chaos reigns.

It would seem that the human intellect is now sufficiently well-cultivated to discern that we are heirs and sharers of the Divine Nature, that our universe is one of law and order, and that all must operate according to law or be destroyed. We should strive to discover the laws that govern our lives so that we can consciously cooperate with those laws.

When the laws are discovered, they should be made a part of the curriculum of every school so that everyone will have the opportunity to learn the proper way to live. Undoubtedly this would bring about a method of cooperation and collaboration that promises a future era in which brotherly love and mutual helpfulness would supplant the evils of today.

Until such knowledge and the urge to cooperate with the Divine in the ceaseless evolution of the Soul does become a part of our educational system, it would be an act of the highest wisdom for us to learn the laws of our being. Then we could begin an active cooperation in order to reach peace, happiness, health and prosperity.

It is written that *"as a man soweth, so shall he also reap."* When we are sufficiently well-versed in the "secrets of life," we can by rigid discipline, under law, enter into and understand what Jesus referred to as *"the Kingdom of God within you."*

CONTENTS

INTRODUCTION

A life of health, happiness, peace, and prosperity is one that we all aspire to live. And it is attainable. Finding the path to that destination—and steadfastly walking it—is, of course, the challenge.

The time-tested truths in *Rays of the Dawn* offer a map that identifies key signposts for the journey. Those signposts are the Natural Laws governing our being, Body, Mind, and Soul. These are not arbitrary Laws. They form the basis for life itself, and are forever in operation. If we learn to follow them, we will unfailingly navigate our way to a better life.

Rays of the Dawn has three parts. Instead of reading it from cover to cover, consider using a strategy that has proven effective for many years. Read all the Laws of the Body in Part One—there are only four—and examine the way you presently nourish, move, rest, and cleanse your body. This may inspire you to make some healthful changes—changes that will clear the way for the next phase of your journey.

As you venture into Parts Two and Three, the Laws of the Mind and Soul, you will notice they are polar opposites:

LAWS OF THE MIND	LAWS OF THE SOUL
Chapter	Chapter
5 .... Fear	17 .... Faith
6 .... Worry	18 .... Hope
7 .... Selfishness	19 .... Generosity
8 .... Vanity	20 .... Aspiration
9 .... Anger	21 .... Patience
10 .... Criticism	22 .... Sympathy
11 .... Envy	23 .... Noninterference
12 .... Greed	24 .... Kindness
13 .... Hypocrisy	25 .... Courage
14 .... Prejudice	26 .... Forgiveness
15 .... Jealousy	27 .... Duty
16 .... Hate	28 .... Love

It is helpful to read these chapters in pairs. Start with any two that you wish, for example, "Hate" and "Love." Read the Law of the Mind, then finish with the corresponding Law of the Soul. Read the pairs in any order you like—just be sure to read them all.

Notice that the Laws governing the Mind are negatives—"Fear," "Worry," "Greed," "Hypocrisy," and so on—while the Laws of the Soul are their positive corollaries: "Faith," "Hope," "Kindness," "Courage," etc. Some honest assessment about the role each plays in your life today may encourage you toward even more positive change.

Every positive change you make will draw you more into harmony with your True Self. It is the inevitable outcome of living in harmony with Natural Law. When that happens, you will seek things that are in harmony with your own nature, rather than things that are contrary to it. Then every aspect of your life will reflect both your True Self and Natural Law.

When Dr. Fleet first presented this material to his patients in the 1930s, society and customs were different from the way they are now. By comparison, today's world moves at a lightning pace, and stress is ever present. Despite the complex differences between then and now, one thing remains the same: people's need for life's truths. For decades, the ageless wisdom in *Rays of the Dawn* has helped people from all walks of life understand themselves, understand others, and build better lives. This same wisdom can help you, too.

The simple fact is that we create our tomorrows by the way we live today, and we live today ruled by our every thought and action. For this reason the journey to health, happiness, peace, and prosperity is different for each of us. However, the destination is most worthy of our effort.

Good luck on your journey!

Part One
THE LAWS OF THE BODY

Chapter One
THE LAW OF NOURISHMENT

The physical part—or body—of every human being is governed by four immutable laws that Nature demands we obey:

The Law of Nourishment

The Law of Movement

The Law of Recuperation

The Law of Sanitation

The first step on the road to total health is to understand and practice these four laws. By doing so we can experience growth as the "inevitable consequence of the undisturbed operation of Nature's Laws."

Much has been said and written concerning food and diet, and it's easy to become confused over the daily choices we must make regarding our nourishment. This chapter should cut through that confusion and help you develop a workable plan for nourishing your body.

Every living organism requires food for its sustenance. Even the simplest vegetable cell takes nourishment and replaces its waste products by taking fresh material into the system. Guided by Innate Intelligence, the plant absorbs the food that is essential for its growth and development. When a plant is grown in a soil and climate conducive to its well-being, Nature produces the finest specimen known. On the other hand, if a plant is grown in impoverished, devitalized soil, it adapts to that environment, becoming a degenerate specimen. The perfect specimen only occurs when allowed to grow and develop in its true environment. In the vegetable kingdom we observe that an Intelligence expressed through natural law guides and controls the sustenance of plants.

Looking at the animal kingdom, we see that the animal, having evolved to a higher state of consciousness than the plant, has tastes and appetites guided by instinct. The animal allowed to roam in a free and natural state is a perfect specimen unless attacked by some outside destructive force. It secures its food in a natural form and eats only when its body requires nourishment. Thus unmolested by the influence of humans, or reason, we find the animal in all its perfection.

When humanity was in a primitive state, we were directed to a great extent by instinct in selecting food and satisfying appetites. As we began to use the new gift, reason, we started to cook, preserve, and concoct our food. We began to tamper with Nature's product, and as a result, destroyed much of its original nutritive value. Consequently, our digestive apparatus has become degenerated, and our food has become deficient in the elements essential to sustain our bodies and maintain health. Only natural food can properly nourish our bodies.

We are far removed from the perfect, natural specimens found in the Garden of Eden. We have disobeyed the Law of Nourishment so long that we don't have perfect digestive organs. They have degenerated due to improper food and wrong living. Therefore, we must modify the Law of Nourishment to pertain to our needs today.

Let's first differentiate between dead, devitalized foods and live foods. Dead foods are those that have been cooked, preserved, or tampered with, destroying some or all of the original vitamin and mineral content. That means any food not in its natural state. Live foods are those that come to us as grown by Nature. It is necessary to preserve some foods, but the fact remains that if we can get natural food, we should use it in preference to the unnatural.

To properly understand foods—their nature, their relation to each other, their function in the human body, their proper combination—we can classify them into four groups: Builders, Eliminators, Congestors, Lubricators. The following analysis includes both dead and live foods.

Group I	Group II	Group III	Group IV
Select one for each meal	Select two for each meal	Eat sparingly at each meal	Use as needed
Builders	**Eliminators**	**Congestors**	**Lubricators**
Avocados	All fresh fruit	All candy	Butter
Beans, lima	except bananas	All cereals	
Beans, kidney		All gum	All oils
Beans, navy	All fresh green	All soft drinks	
Beef	vegetables	containing	All fats
Butter (also 4)		sugar	
Cheese	Canned/frozen	Anything made	
Eggs	spinach	from flour	
Fish		Bananas	
Fowl	Canned/frozen	Bread	
Lamb	tomatoes	Cake	
Lentils		Dried fruits	
Milk		Flour	
Mushrooms		Gravies made	
Nuts		from flour	
Pork		Honey	
		Jams	
		Jellies	
		Macaroni	
		Molasses	
		Noodles	
		Potatoes	
		Old corn	
		Spaghetti	

Group I—Builders

These foods build the body. They are acid-forming, however, so we should eat enough but not too much of this group. In general we should eat at least one building food per day. The great majority of us can eat one kind at each meal. Building foods include: all nuts, avocados, milk, eggs, dried peas, dried lima beans, mushrooms, dried kidney beans, dried navy beans, dried lentils, butter, cheese, fish, fowl, beef, pork, lamb—and all other flesh foods.

Group II—Eliminators

These foods tear down, repair, and eliminate the waste material from the body. They tear down that part of the body that needs to be torn down. Always eat three times as much of this food as the building food. Everyone should have some of Group II with every meal. Eliminative foods include the following fruits: lemons, limes, grapefruits, oranges, pineapples, peaches, cherries, apricots, plums, apples, pears, blackberries, raspberries, strawberries, cranberries, currants, gooseberries, cantaloupes, muskmelon, honeydew melon, watermelon, tomatoes—and all other fruits except bananas.

Group II also includes these vegetables: celery, spinach, endive, lettuce, carrots, asparagus, dandelion, parsley, swiss chard, onions, beets, green peppers, peas, cucumbers, raw cabbage, cauliflower, string beans, artichokes, summer squash—and all other vegetables except avocados, dried beans, dried peas and potatoes. These last three contain too much starch and are not eliminative foods. Avocados contain protein and fat and are in Group I.

Group III—Congestors

These are the sweets and starches. Their function is to prevent oxygen from remaining in insoluble combinations with minerals during energy release. Do not eat an over-amount of sweets and starches because they cause congestion.

Starches include: Irish potatoes, sweet potatoes, all breads, all cakes, macaroni, noodles, spaghetti, flour, gravies made with flour, anything made from flour, all cereals and old corn.

Sweets include: all sugars, bananas, pumpkin, squash (Hubbard), honey, molasses, all dried fruits, all candy, all gum, all soft drinks containing sugar, all canned fruits containing sugar, jams, jellies—anything containing sugar.

Group IV—Lubricators

This group includes all vegetable oils, olive oil, butter, and fats. These foods build and lubricate. If you are too thin, eat freely of these foods; if too fat, use them sparingly.

Special Tips

- Most people eat too much starch. That is the reason we have so much sinus trouble, constipation, colds, asthma, whooping cough, colitis, and diseases of congestion.
- Many people eat too many acid-forming foods. This is the cause underlying so much arthritis, rheumatism, neuritis, aches in the joints, eczema, skin trouble, etc.
- The water used in cooking vegetables should not be thrown away as it contains the mineral salts. Drink it as soup.
- Do not eat unless you have a natural craving for food. If you aren't hungry, omit a meal and allow your natural appetite to return.

Planning Balanced Menus

A well balanced meal should comprise:

- One kind of food from Group I (the base of the meal)
- Two kinds from Group II
- One kind from Group III (only if hungry)
- Use Group IV if needed

You can easily divide the meal into three courses:

- First—Group I, Builders
- Second—Group II, Eliminators
- Third—Group III, Congestors (only if still hungry)
- Use Group IV when needed

The following menus are correctly combined, balanced meals. Use these or make up your own.*

BREAKFASTS (read across)

Group I	Group II	Group III	Group IV
2 poached or coddled eggs	1/2 grapefruit	1 slice toast	Butter
Eggs	Dish of prunes	Toast	Cream
Cheddar cheese	Apples or other fresh fruit	Crackers	Butter
1 handful shelled nuts	Pineapple juice or sweet fruit	Whole wheat cereal (dry)	Cream
Scrambled eggs	Orange juice	1 slice toast	Butter
2 soft boiled eggs	Baked apple	Toast	Butter Cream
Cottage cheese	Fresh pineapple or other fresh fruit in season	Crackers or Ry-Crisp	Butter
Eggs & bacon (crisp)	Tomato juice	1 slice toast	Butter
	Fresh or canned sweet fruit	Maple syrup, whole wheat waffles	Butter
	Stewed or fresh fruit	Cereal	Cream

LUNCHEONS (read across)

Group I	Group II	Group III	Group IV
Lamb chops	Fruit cup, lettuce & tomato salad	Baked potato	Butter
Omelette	Orange juice or grapefruit	Ry-Crisp or toast	Butter
Half avocado	Lettuce, celery, olives, lemon	Crackers	Salad dressing
Cottage cheese	Sliced pineapple or other fruit	Toast or crackers	Butter
Lima beans	Combination salad, buttered beets	Whole wheat crackers	Butter, salad oil
Cheese	Stuffed celery, lettuce or water-cress, fruit or tomato juice	1 slice bread	Butter Mayonnaise
Tuna fish salad	Pineapple or lemon, lettuce, celery, olives	Crackers	Butter, salad dressing
Handful of nuts	Combination salad of fresh vegetables, lemon juice		Olive oil
Custard	Vegetable Plate	Baked potato	Butter

DINNERS (read across)

Group I	Group II	Group III	Group IV
Baked fish	Lettuce and tomato salad, lemon, string beans	Baked potato	Butter Mayonnaise
Roast meat or fowl	Cranberries, celery, spinach, tomato juice	Dressing for the meat, potatoes	Butter

DINNERS cont. (read across)

Group I	Group II	Group III	Group IV
Pea soup	Fruit salad, celery, olives	Macaroni and cheese	Butter, salad dressing
Liver	Tomato juice, combination vegetable salad, onions	1 slice bread	Butter
Broiled steak	Tomato juice or vegetable cocktail, buttered beets or green peas, fruit whip or fruit Jell-O	Baked potatoes or yams	Butter
Omelette	Half grapefruit or tomato juice, peas and carrots, celery hearts	Potato salad	Salad dressing
Lima beans or baked beans	Lettuce, stuffed tomatoes	Dried fruit	Salad dressing

There is no field of science more exploited by theorists and commercial faddists than that of nutrition. With all the theories and fads in circulation regarding food and the proper combination of food—what to eat and what not to eat—it's no wonder that the average person is hopelessly confused. Often that person will go to a doctor in quest of reliable information.

Anyone with a normal digestive system can eat good wholesome food properly combined. The Intelligence within the body is the chemist that extracts from that food all the chemicals, minerals, and vitamins essential for health and vitality.

There are two extremes in combining foods. Exponents of one extreme limit their diet to natural foods only. The followers of the other combine their meals without any regard for dietetic rules. A good compromise between these two is to properly and sensibly balance each meal for health, according to the Law of Nourishment.

* The Concept-Therapy Institute publishes *Balanced Meals*, a booklet of scientifically combined, easy-to-follow menus, and the companion pamphlet, *Inner-Klean Diet: A Six-Day Diet to Remove Toxins from the Body*. To order, please see "For More Information" in the back of this book.

Chapter Two
THE LAW OF MOVEMENT

When we live in ignorance and defiance of Nature's laws we lead false, artificial lives. In order for life to be progressive, it must be natural. Nature demands obedience to her laws, or she will gradually but surely eliminate those of us who violate them. When we know, understand, and obey the Law of Movement, our lives and health take on a different expression.

Our bodies must absorb and distribute the nourishment contained in the food we eat. If we consume the proper food, thereby complying with the Law of Nourishment, but our bodies are unable to absorb it, then ill health will inevitably follow. If our bodies can absorb the nourishment but cannot distribute it, ill health will also result. These laws are absolute. Movement, or exercise, is the only distributing agent of our bodies.

The Creative Intelligence that planned and made our bodies intended that we should be able to obey the Law of Movement, and to that end the Creative Intelligence gave us joints and muscles intended to be moved. When we exercise these joints and muscles sufficiently, the nutrition that we get from our food is distributed, by being moved, to all parts of the body. Many people have stiff backs, stiff legs, stiff arms, necks, fingers, and hips, etc., because they have ceased to move them and to care for them intelligently. They have been violating Nature's laws. Such people may continue in their violation for a certain period of time, but eventually Nature will eliminate them.

Much erroneous information has been circulated regarding the kind and amount of exercise that an individual should take.

Exercise is dangerous, unless it is based on truth, common sense, and knowledge of a person's physical and mental condition. There are a great many people engaged in selling exercise programs that really do a great deal of harm to thousands of individuals every year. Prescribing a system of exercises to millions of people is just as unscientific as prescribing cooked cabbage to those same millions. What lay person or doctor can intelligently tell another person what he or she should do in terms of artificial exercise without ever seeing or knowing the physical condition of that individual?

Natural movement can be prescribed to any human being alive, because it complies with the Law of Movement, but artificial movement (exercise) can be injurious. Exercise, like everything else concerning a human body, is an individual matter. What is indicated for one person may be all out of order—even harmful—for another unless it is a system where individuality predominates.

To know and understand what is required for obedience to Nature's Law of Movement, we must know:
- Why our joints should be moved
- When our joints should be moved
- Which of our joints should be moved
- How our joints should be moved

Why Move Our Joints?

Joints should be moved for the simple reason that they are designed for use and movement. If we use and move them and care for them intelligently they will become strong and healthy. Otherwise, they will soon lose their strength and power of movement. This law is absolute.

To illustrate, assume that a man tied his left arm to his side so that it couldn't be moved, and kept it that way for one year. Then, when he did untie the arm and try to move it, it would not move. The muscles, due to inactivity, had lost their tone. The joints were stiff. He did not comply with Nature's Law of Movement, and the Intelligence within his body gradually but surely started to eliminate that arm.

Ask yourself: Do I have any movable joints in my body that are stiff and sore when I try to move them? If you do, then that is conclusive proof that you have been disobeying the Law of Movement, and the soreness you feel is part of the penalty that you are beginning to pay.

Now stand erect and start moving your eyes, neck, shoulders, elbows, fingers, hips, knees, ankles, toes, spine, etc., and determine for yourself if you can move them every way they were intended to move without pain. If any of these parts produce pain upon movement, that is an indication that they are abnormal. You should resort to the necessary therapeutic measures in order to bring these parts back to normal.

When Should We Move Them?

We should move our joints sufficiently every day. If we lived a natural life, as we were intended to live, we would be compelled to move all of our joints. But we live in an unnatural environment—confined to cities, buying our food instead of raising it or hunting for it, riding in automobiles instead of walking and running, staying up late at night instead of lying down to rest and sleep when darkness arrives, eating artificial and dead, devitalized food instead of natural, live food. Therefore, having reduced bodily movements to a minimum, we are compelled to resort to artificial movement or exercise in order to keep our joints in good order.

As soon as you have moved your joints sufficiently, you will experience a feeling of tiredness in the muscles or in the joints being moved. That feeling of tiredness is a message from the Intelligence within to stop exercising. Only you can determine when you have had enough exercise, and only you—or someone thoroughly familiar with your physical condition—can prescribe the kind of exercise you can take.

What would happen if a man with arthritis subscribed to a commercial exercise program saying he should walk five miles a day, bend down and touch the floor with his fingers twenty times in succession, hop on one leg ten minutes and then to hop on the other leg ten minutes? What would happen to a woman suffering from a stiff neck if she should indulge in a program that states she should rotate her neck as far as it will go, backwards, forwards, sideways—forty times each day?

Which Joints Should We Move?

All movable joints should be moved—jaw, shoulders, hands, hips, neck, elbows, fingers, knees, feet, toes, chest (by deep breathing), wrists, ankles, and the entire spine. When we move all these parts sufficiently, until tiredness develops, we are moving all the muscles attached to them, and nutrition is being evenly distributed to all parts of our bodies.

The exercise faddists make their mistake when they try to develop some muscle at the expense of others and at great expense to the heart. Many people following those programs do develop great strength in some of the muscles, but some other part of the body pays the price. What do people gain by developing great strength in their arms, legs, and chest if they have weakened their hearts?

How Should We Move Them?

Exercise is good and it is necessary for health, particularly for the lungs and heart. Yet too much or too strenuous an exercise program will cause heart disease and destroy the lungs. Excess is harmful and moderation is beneficial. In both work and play we must use the Law of Movement, but there is much difference between the two. Some tell us that work is a task, a duty, and therefore unpleasant. But that is not true. When the body is in good physical and mental condition, work is a pleasure.

Play relieves our working muscles by using them in a different way or by relaxing them when used with other muscles. A letter carrier would not consider walking a pleasure, but a boy who sawed wood would consider painting a fence the height of sport. It is change that pleases. The spirit of anticipation adds zest and, as long as it continues, our muscles will respond to the demands we make on them. When anticipation ceases, the muscles are tired and that is the signal to stop.

Good times to exercise are just before going to bed and upon arising. Stand up straight and begin moving your eyes every way they will move until tiredness develops. Then move your jaw every way it will move until tiredness develops. Open a window—do not stand in a draft—and draw in deep breaths. Inhale and exhale until tiredness develops. Then move your shoulders, elbows, wrists, hands, fingers. Exercise the twenty-five joints of the spine by bending forward and backward and from side to side until tiredness develops. Place your hands on your hips and rotate your hips backward, forward, and from side to side until they feel tired. Continue by moving the knees, ankles, feet and toes, etc.

Observe these two simple rules:

1. Move every movable joint every way that it will move until tiredness develops.

2. If pain develops in any joint during movement, do not continue the movement past the point where pain develops. Gradually the pain will diminish.

Don't indulge in any exercise program that prescribes moving this way so many times and that way so many times, because the simple truth is that every human being is different. What will apply to you will not be indicated for someone else. The Intelligence within the body—which created the body and governs it (when allowed to do so)—is the only judge as to how much exercise is required for that body. Exercise will create tiredness when you have given the joints and muscles sufficient movement, and that is the stop signal.

Comply with the Law of Movement, and give every movable joint sufficient movement every day.

Chapter Three
THE LAW OF RECUPERATION

There is a great Natural Law that demands of every living creature a sufficient amount of rest and sleep. During this period of inactivity, the forces of the body endeavor to repair the damage that has been done throughout the day. Every human being and every animal must obey this law in some degree because continuous, never-ceasing activity—for any living thing—means untimely death.

To recuperate means to recover, and in this law it means to recover the energy expended during the day. There are three ways to recuperate: rest, recreation, and sleep.

Rest

Rest is the most important element in a life of healthful living. Even when we are hard at work, we need frequent breathing spells and changes of occupation and amusement to keep our muscles and our minds in a healthy condition. Even the strongest and hardiest of us cannot continue indefinitely in an unbroken line of endeavor. There comes a time when mere sitting still will not rest us. Then, sleep is needed to restore the body.

Nature has provided for alternate activity and rest. Rest is the counterpoise of movement or exercise. In the vegetable kingdom we see no apparent cessation of activity. Plants are stationary, not subject to voluntary motion. No movement is initiated from within except the phenomena of growth, preservation, and reproduction. These activities are all purely physiological. Thus, plant life is governed only by physiological rest. We see plants and even seeds going through periods of activity and dormancy. Possessing no muscular system, plants don't engage in muscular activity. The neural or conscious activity manifest in some forms of highly developed plant life is not sufficient to call for rest.

To maintain health and vitality, both humans and animals must obey the Law of Recuperation. Animals are subject to the Law of Movement, therefore, they must obey the Law of Recuperation. Because they engage in neural and muscular activity, animals must rest and sleep. An instinctive force directs animals in search of food, water, and building material for their homes, or they may be driven about, or frightened away from their abodes, by some outside force. Thus animals stay in motion. As long as their activity is not interfered with by man's reason, animals will obey the Law of Recuperation. They will rest after action. When the task is completed or the chase is ended, animals will lie down and rest, though they may not sleep. Some animals sleep or rest during the day and go on the hunt at night. Others prolong their rest periods and hibernate for a season. Although animals may engage in some mental activity, this is of a purely sensuous nature, and therefore requires only physical rest.

Humans, with our highly developed muscular and nervous systems, must obey all three phases of the Law of Recuperation: rest, recreation, and sleep. To fully understand this law, we should know why, when, what, and how we should rest:

- We should rest for the simple reason that we get tired. Tiredness is a signal from the Intelligence within that activity should cease, as harm is being done. If we don't rest when we feel this tiredness, greater harm is being done.

- We should rest when we are conscious of being tired—or as soon after as possible.
- We should rest the entire body or any part that is tired.
- We should rest by putting the body or any part of it that is tired in a position where it relaxes completely.

Whenever we exercise or engage in any type of physical activity, we consume energy and muscular power. These sources of power must be replenished at intervals so that the body can function effectively. Even though we rest the physical part of our bodies, many of the physiological processes don't cease as they must continue in their function until death. But during periods of rest, the strain on such organs and muscles as the heart and lungs is lessened, and thus they are strengthened for further activity.

When humanity was endowed with reason and the power of choice, we began to indulge in mental activity of a very complex nature. We use and often overtax our brains. Thus it is evident that we must have not only physical and physiological rest, but also periods when we cease all mental concentration. Unless this mental or brain activity ceases at times—or is changed to lesser forms of activity—the mind becomes a parasite on the body and the whole organism suffers. The brain must relax; we must have a diversion from work.

People who overindulge in physical activity deplete their physical strength and overdraw on the supply of energy required to carry on the physiological processes. Those who allow their brains to work day and night without cessation will eventually deplete their nervous energy. Consequently, they will suffer impaired health and low vitality. Such individuals soon become a bundle of nerves, suffer from nervous exhaustion, and are the victims of all types of physical and mental disorders.

Even if we don't completely cease concentrated mental effort, we can find an outlet in a change of activity or in some form of recreation—the second phase of the Law of Recuperation.

Recreation

Recreation is essential to maintain healthful and wholesome living, but it is not a substitute for rest. Recreation differs from rest, because it is activity which calls into action parts of the body or brain not ordinarily used. Or it uses parts previously active in a different manner: It recreates by a change of activity.

We should indulge in recreation frequently because it rests the mind and certain muscles of the body. Freeing the mind from the strain of daily tasks and the responsibilities of life has untold benefits. Therefore, every one of us should participate in some form of amusement daily. Everyone should have a hobby. Latent talents and abilities often find expression through hobbies. Within each of us is an urge for self-expression. This urge often finds an outlet in hobbies, because the routine of daily work may not present such opportunities.

Through recreation we can balance our program of daily activity. The nerves and muscles that have been actively engaged in routine work are allowed to rest, and those that have been inactive or dormant are stimulated and set into motion. Thus we see that by changing the nature of our activity, we can reduce the amount of rest required. We must not make the mistake, however, of over-indulging in recreation and reducing the amount of necessary sleep. Also, we should not allow our participation in hobbies, sports, and other forms of recreation to become a dissipation of energies essential for efficiency in work.

Sleep

Sleep, the third phase of recuperation, is a natural temporary period of almost complete unconsciousness, normally occurring at night, in which the body rests. During sleep voluntary muscular activity ceases except for slight unconscious movements. However, the involuntary muscles controlling the processes of circulation, respiration, digestion, etc., continue in their activity, although at a lessened or slower pace.

When the body falls asleep, the conscious mind also rests. Frequently the thoughts and problems that we have concentrated on during waking hours pass into the subconscious and become the subject of our dreams. Sometimes we awaken with the solution to a problem that had weighed on the conscious mind during a previous day's activity. Thus we see that although sleep is a state of rest or freedom from physical and mental effort, still it is not complete. Many of our functions and activities—physical, mental, and physiological—continue during sleep.

To maintain health and vitality, every one of us must secure a sufficient amount of sleep. This period of rest restores the fatigued body to normal. It reinvigorates our muscles, nerves, and glands for further activity. Our mental capacity is renewed and refreshed. Just how much sleep a person needs is an individual matter, but we should awaken feeling rested and rejuvenated. Eight hours is considered the normal amount of sleep for the average person. However, some of us may require more and others less, depending on our physical status, nervous temperament, age, and the type of activity engaged in during waking hours. People who do not obtain sufficient sleep become nervous and irritable, impairing their health and happiness.

Nature demands sleep. It is the only way that the forces of the body and mind can successfully repair the damage done during the day. Much reconstructive work occurs during sleep. Not only are both body and mind replenished and strengthened to continue functioning effectively, but much waste material is also eliminated during this period of freedom from tension. When mind and body are relaxed, Nature can more easily eliminate acids and toxins from the system. Thus sleep provides a time for our bodies to detoxify and alkalinize.

To ensure restful sleep, mind and body must be completely relaxed. People who know how to relax, physically and mentally, require less rest during the day and find it easy to slip off into slumber at night. Those whose activities are characterized by haste, turmoil, and confusion dissipate much valuable energy. We must control and keep at a minimum the hurry and tension of modern day living in order to conserve the energy needed to carry on the vital functions of both mind and body.

When lying down to rest or sleep, we should clear the mind of all thoughts and relax every part of the body completely. Relaxation provides for complete rest and induces sound sleep. If we cannot sleep well, there is something wrong with our health or with our habits. Insomnia is a danger signal to be heeded at once.

Generally speaking, there are two main causes for sleeplessness: physical disturbance or mental disturbance. Both of these can be intelligently eliminated. We can usually attribute an inability to sleep to a lack of physical exercise and an overindulgence in the destructive emotions, especially fear and worry. People cannot expect to sleep if they have not exerted themselves sufficiently to require rest, or if they are emotionally disturbed. Also, if they are physically ill, they usually experience a corresponding mental depression with its accompanying states of fear and worry.

To eliminate the mental causes of insomnia, we must usually make a corresponding change in our physical condition and activities. When our minds are daily occupied in constructive work and when we seek diversion in outdoor activities, we rarely suffer from insomnia. Not only does such activity produce a tiredness in our muscles but it also provides an outlet for mental energy and tension. A brisk walk in the open air will also relax tense muscles and nerves and is conducive to restful sleep. Those who have difficulty sleeping should eat lightly in the evenings. A loaded stomach in a tired body will interfere with sleep—or at least keep the sleep from being as beneficial as when digestion is not taxed.

Proper ventilation is most important during sleep. We should sleep in a room that has plenty of fresh air, but not in a draft. Where climate and circumstances permit, sleeping out-of-doors is very beneficial. We should assume a position that is most comfortable, and one that produces the greatest relaxation.

Generally speaking, everyone should secure plenty of sleep. Only you yourself can know when you have had a sufficient amount. Everyone should indulge in good, clean recreation—such as movies, games, amusements, hobbies, etc.—and have plenty of rest in order to comply with Nature's Law of Recuperation.

Chapter Four
THE LAW OF SANITATION

Cleanliness is indispensable in keeping our bodies healthy, wholesome, and beautiful. Not only does cleanliness affect the body but it also reaches to the confines of the mind, the soul, and the Spirit. Since the body is the abode of the mind and the soul, and the instrument of the Spirit, these can evolve to higher planes of existence only in an environment that is clean and pure.

If we were living in a natural state, we would scarcely have to concern ourselves with the Law of Sanitation, for Nature would take care of us. But we live artificially—we are exposed to an unnatural environment—and we violate the other three Laws of the body: Nourishment, Movement, and Recuperation. Therefore, we must obey the Law of Sanitation to maintain any degree of health and wholesomeness.

External Cleanliness

Think of the human body as having two sides, the outside and the inside. Both must be kept clean or we reap ill health and disease. External cleanliness affects not only the purity of our blood but our general internal wholesomeness.

The outside of our bodies is covered with tiny pores called sweat glands. These tiny pores constantly eliminate waste material that the Intelligence within the body cannot utilize and is trying to dispose of. Were we living in a natural state, we would not wear clothing, and our skin would be exposed to the sun's rays, which in turn would absorb the poison being eliminated. But clothing interferes with the natural functioning of our pores, so we must resort to using soap and water to remove the daily accumulation of poisons.

If these poisons, which are continually being eliminated, are not washed off, they harden and clog our pores. Then the balance of the toxins in the system cannot be discharged. Thus our bodies become poisoned by the very poison that the Intelligence is trying to eliminate. For this reason bathing once or twice a week is insufficient. We should bathe daily with soap and water. In general, our physical condition, diet, and activities should determine the amount of bathing we need.

The farther we allow our bodies to deviate from a state of physical perfection, the greater the accumulation of acids and toxins in the bloodstream, and the greater the burden placed on the eliminative organs in Nature's effort to expel these poisons. Consequently, there is a greater need for bathing to insure external cleanliness and enable the pores of the skin to perform their function effectively.

When bathing just remember that the temperature of the body is 98.6° . If we jump into water that is too hot or too cold, we immediately shock the inside and the outside of the body. As a result, the entire system compensates for this shock by working hard to maintain normal temperature—and a considerable harm can occur. As a precautionary measure, have your bath water about the same temperature as your body, or just a few degrees higher, and then gradually change to hot or cold if desired. This does not mean that hot and cold baths are not recommended. Both have their merits, but approach them gradually.

A hot bath is more cleansing than a cold one and is especially useful when our pores are clogged with dirt and grease due to exposure. Not only do hot baths open and cleanse our pores but they further facilitate the elimination of poisons by inducing perspiration. The hot bath tends to relax, whereas the cold bath is stimulating. However, the neutral bath is often preferable to either, especially when our vitality is low or if we suffer from a nervous condition. In contrast, cold baths are invaluable for their invigorating and toning effects on the whole system.

External cleanliness involves not only our skin but also our hair, nails, mouth, teeth. It also pertains to those things in our immediate environment that we come in contact with: clothing, food, dishes, bedding, etc. It is just as important to keep our hair, nails, mouth, and teeth sanitary as it is to bathe daily. Hygiene habits should be developed in little children, so those habits will become routine throughout their adult lives.

Internal Cleanliness

If our diet consists of natural foods correctly combined, our bodies will naturally cleanse themselves. A diet consisting chiefly of fruits and vegetables balanced by sufficient building foods, whole grains, and lubricating foods will not only nourish our bodies but will, at the same time, insure proper elimination. Fruits and vegetables have a flushing and cleansing effect that eliminates waste material. They also possess the necessary cellulose to exercise and tone up the whole digestive and eliminative tract. Whole grains also provide the necessary bulk, and in addition are one of the richest sources of vitamin B, which is so essential in maintaining normal elimination.

Living as most of us do on dead, artificial foods, we quite naturally produce death inside our bodies. This death is exceedingly difficult to get rid of. We eat food that congests our entire system, and as a result we become constipated. When our bowels fail to move, we resort to using high-powered laxatives, and again we harm the body. Very often we find that these laxatives lose their power. Then we resort to using enemas to secure elimination. Laxatives will never cure constipation, and their continued use only aggravates the condition. Using enemas to secure elimination is a most unnatural procedure and should be confined to emergencies only. Their constant use will soon weaken and balloon the bowels, leading to further intestinal trouble.

Constipation has various causes, but fundamentally results from our failing to obey the Laws of Nourishment, Movement, and Recuperation. In times past, doctors and health authorities held that constipation was due to a lack of exercise and lack of fiber in the diet. With the discovery of vitamins, however, came proof that intestinal stasis, in many instances, is caused by a deficiency of vitamin B, especially B1. It is therefore essential that our daily diets contain sufficient food sources of vitamin B, including whole grain. Anyone who cannot tolerate these foods should supplement with the vitamin B complex.

We should not overlook exercise as an essential factor in insuring internal cleanliness. People who never exercise lack strength and tone in their abdominal muscles. This weakness often leads to constipation. We must indulge in a certain amount of physical activity to induce perspiration, which in turn assists our pores in eliminating poisons. Without perspiration, our kidneys carry a greater load in throwing off poisons that were not eliminated through our skin. Furthermore, normal circulation depends on exercise, and without proper circulation our blood cannot carry waste products to our eliminative organs for disposal.

Nervous tension is another source of intestinal stasis. Conversely, intestinal trouble causes nervous tension. Constant physical and mental nervous tension affects all our bodily organs, especially the endocrine glands. We must obey the Law of Recuperation to insure proper digestion and elimination, thus providing internal cleanliness.

Our minds play an important role in the source of constipation. Destructive emotions such as worry, hatred, fear—all thoughts of that nature—will directly or indirectly interfere with our digestive organs' normal functions, thus paving the way for an unwholesome internal condition.

Although water is important in maintaining internal cleanliness, it is erroneous to believe that by drinking large quantities of water we can cleanse the system of its waste material. Water only flushes. It never cleanses unless combined with alkaline elements that will dissolve the acids and toxins so they can be absorbed by the bloodstream and excreted. Natural fluids, especially fruit and vegetable juices, not only supply the body with the necessary liquid but they also enrich the bloodstream. That promotes all functions of the body, especially the elimination of wastes. The amount of water each of us requires depends on such factors as climatic conditions, diet, exercise or labor, and fluids we take in other forms.

Adequate elimination is essential for preserving health, and this means elimination through every eliminative channel—kidneys, bowels, skin, and lungs. Our bowels should evacuate never less than twice a day on an ample diet. However, three evacuations a day are preferable. It is a well-known fact that after we place food in our mouths, it takes a certain length of time to pass through our digestive tracts before being eliminated. It follows, then, that if we eat three meals a day, we should have three bowel movements a day. If we have only one, we can be certain that the other two remain inside too long, and part of the toxins are being reabsorbed. If we comply with the Laws of Nourishment, Movement, and Recuperation—and comply with them long enough—our elimination will be normal.

Part Two
THE LAWS OF THE MIND

Chapter Five
FEAR

The wise man seeketh that which is in harmony with his own nature and endeavors to fit his life accordingly, rather than to seek after things contrary to his nature. – Bhagavad Gita (Yogi Ramacharka)

Each of us has a body, a mind, and a soul. In order to maintain a perfect state of health, it is necessary for us to obey the laws of Nature governing these parts. Having completed the laws that govern the human body, we can now consider the mind and its faculties in their relation to health. By analyzing the destructive forces that operate in the mind, we can show their action and just why they should be eliminated.

The first destructive force to consider is that of fear. Fear in the mind disturbs the entire makeup of a human being—body, mind, and soul. Fear paralyzes growth, and therefore should be controlled. After acquiring knowledge of the law involved, we will no longer allow fear to rule or disrupt our being. And in the degree that we liberate ourselves from the bondage of fear, we will enjoy greater health and happiness, and a greater peace of mind. Deliverance from fear releases the powers within that promote development of the whole organism.

Fear is the antithesis of faith. It is based on a lack of confidence or an apprehension of danger, unhappiness, doubt, anxiety, worry, dread, hatred, anger, horror, fright, shock, terror. All these emotions are direct results of the different phases of fear. Each shares the general characteristics of the state known as *being afraid of some thing, person, influence or action not desired and hence feared in direct ratio to its undesirability.*

FEAR ⇌ **FAITH**

Our mental state is frequently the result of thinking about a fear in regard to its probable effect on our own happiness—or perhaps indirectly, on the life of another. It is an emotional state of mental disquiet, unrest, unease, which is dis-ease wrongly called *disease*. Through a knowledge of the laws governing the mind, the mind has control over itself and over the body. It can intelligently carry the body safely through many occurrences that would otherwise create an unhealthy state and eventually result in an untimely death. Chaos and fear in our thoughts will produce suffering and disease in our bodies.

Experiments with animals have shown that under pressure of fear the whole metabolic process is disturbed. It retards—and in some cases halts—the digestive and assimilative functions. Other physiological processes alter or accelerate. It stimulates the heart, lungs, and adrenal glands to greater activity. The abdominal arteries constrict, thereby forcing large quantities of blood to other parts of the body, especially the lungs, brain, skin, and skeletal muscles. Thus we see that the emotion of fear prepares the individual, human or animal, for the greatest muscular strength and endurance.

Fear is a stimulus to action, and the individual instinctively prepares for fight or flight. Primitive humans found an outlet for this preparatory energy by contending with human and animal enemies and with natural forces that were hostile to their well-being. In modern life these preparatory reactions do not always find expression in physical exertion. In fact, such expression is a rare occurrence. When we fail to act, fear becomes inverted, for that which cannot go outward must go inward. Thus we create panic within, and our whole organism is disturbed.

Fear is our greatest enemy, with all the evils of doubt, uncertainty, and apprehension that follow in its wake. To eliminate or at least control fear, we must conquer it. To conquer fear, we must face it. Fear is a challenge that we must meet.

It has been said that we find our significance by *working through difficulty*, not by cringing in its presence. Whenever fear presents itself, it should be met, analyzed and, if possible, intelligently eliminated. If we cannot perform some intelligent activity when confronted with fear, then we should do something foolish—but action is imperative.

Activity obscures the emotion of fear by bringing our thought processes and other constructive emotions into play. Furthermore, activity liberates and utilizes pent-up energy. Indecision leads to perdition. It is better to make a wrong move and later rectify the mistake than to remain undecided as to what course of action to pursue.

There are thousands in our hospitals who are suffering from physical and mental disorders—thousands whose minds and bodies are wrecked—because they have not learned to rid themselves of needless fears. They and their doctors are more concerned with treating the effects than with eliminating the cause of their illness: the demon of fear. Also, some doctors commonly use fear as a weapon to coerce patients into following instructions and, in some instances, into continuing needless treatment. Worse, there are parents who instill fear in the minds of children to force them to obey certain rules of conduct.

Frequently a patient will come to a doctor for treatment, and although concerned about a condition, the patient harbors no fear. The doctor, however, wanting to impress the patient with the seriousness of the condition, instills the fear of death in an untroubled mind.

To illustrate, let's assume a woman is suffering from high

blood pressure and goes to her doctor for treatment. Being unaware of the nature of her illness, she suffers only physically from it. The doctor, doing what in his ignorance he thinks is right, places fear in her mind. He impresses her with the seriousness of her condition, saying that high blood pressure often results in paralysis. The patient remembers having heard that people die with high blood pressure, so fear, terrible fear, enters her mind. Now she suffers mentally as well as physically from her illness.

Instead of co-ordinating the body and mind into a cure, the doctor did just the opposite, thereby making the patient a great deal worse. Further, the fear generated in her mind brought on other physical symptoms: loss of appetite, wrinkles, loss of energy, etc. This fear completely upset her mind.

The patient's subconscious mind was impressed to the extent that even though she did recover eventually from the high blood pressure, there would have been a *fear complex* in her makeup that would have disturbed her entire organism. It would have remained in her subconscious until such time as it would have been intelligently removed.

The intelligent doctor is cautious and tactful in presenting the facts to a patient and does not unduly alarm the person regarding any condition. Such a doctor would have told our hypothetical patient that her blood pressure is too high but that it is not considered dangerous—provided she uses her intelligence and obeys the simple laws involved in high blood pressure while the doctor is intelligently doing something to reduce the blood pressure.

The doctor then truthfully, forcefully, intelligently, and logically explains the laws involved and explains what can be done to remove the condition. When the patient sees, knows, understands, and believes that what the doctor has told her is, in fact, a truth, then, and only then, will she reason on this truth and quite naturally conclude that she can get well.

Fear is a destructive emotion. Anyone who suffers from it should know and comply with the laws governing fear:

1. Find out what it is that causes you to fear.
2. Eliminate the fear through intelligent action.
3. If it is not within your power to eliminate the fear, then consult someone who has made a study of the human mind. Present your case to the doctor, or mental healer, who in turn will analyze this fear. Then, using your intelligence and willpower, eliminate the fear.
4. Do not fear anything needlessly. Analyze your fears in the light of truth, and you will find that there is, in reality, nothing worthy of being feared.

In eliminating fear we must learn that the trials of life are not motiveless. The problems and difficulties that we must face and overcome are really incentives to further human development. Appearing as ugly excrescences on the path of life, they are in reality the stepping stones to better things. We must have the bad in order to appreciate the good. Real happiness comes to us through struggling with the difficult and overcoming it.

Fear is only a beacon that warns us of impending danger. To allow fear to absorb and control our nature merely indicates that we are the victim of negative thinking. When we think negatively, we attract to ourselves those forces that are destructive to our being. Fear is a signal to withdraw to safety or to call upon Divine Guidance for protection—to know that no evil can befall us. The universe is one of law, order, and harmony and is not the result of mere chance or accident. Accidents and misfortunes are not the normal outcome of our experience and

FEAR ⟺ FAITH

do not constitute a part of the Divine Plan.

There are many types of fear. Psychologically speaking, most of them are unconscious. Some of our fears originate in childhood experiences; others originate from ancestral memories that are hidden and obscured in the subconscious. In our conscious and waking state, we must strive to bring these experiences and memories to the threshold of consciousness to eliminate the negative thought patterns, thus freeing ourselves from the domination of fear.

To free ourselves of fear's bondage is, indeed, a great victory. But as long as we are slaves to the illusion of the pair of opposites—such as good and evil, love and hate, life and death—we will be imprisoned by our thought. Once we see the opposites in their true light, we rise above them and harmonize ourselves with the Divine. Harmonizing with the Divine indicates that we have attained to wisdom, and that destructive emotions are no longer capable of disturbing our consciousness.

Chapter Six
WORRY

The second destructive force of the human mind is worry. Here we must differentiate between good healthy planning or constructive thinking and the destructive state of mind manifesting in the form of nervous anxiety or mental distress. In this case the word *worry* means: A *destructive state of mind manifested in the form of mental distress concerning some person, thing, circumstance, problem, condition, or situation, and associated with the emotional state of apprehension, fear, anxiety, dread, or regret.*

It is a psychological fact that thoughts must be either positive or negative. Negative thinking results in real disease or disturbed mentality, either of which destroys health and happiness. Worry, being negative, is an enemy and should be eliminated. If we allow worry to dominate our consciousness, intelligence becomes submerged. Only when we use our God-given reason are we able to remove this useless and antagonistic force from our consciousness. Not only is worry a diseased condition of consciousness but, interfering as it does with the normal functions of the bodily organs, it causes many physical diseases, and also many mental disorders of varying kind and degree.

Worry depends on an incorrect interpretation in our consciousness. As humanity evolves to a higher state of existence—becoming more civilized and thoughtful, living less in the present and more in the past and future—the human nervous system undergoes a higher organization and becomes more sensitive, resulting in susceptibility to a disturbed condition of the mind. In this respect, we are more subject to worry and its effects than any organism of a lower order of intelligence.

Each of us must, of necessity, experience obstacles, problems, difficulties, disappointments, and thwarted plans. These things are but challenges that we must meet. Either we must conquer them through elimination or adaptation, or else we become their victims and are subdued.

A first law of growth requires that surroundings suit the needs of species and organisms, or else distortion and death follow. It is paramount, therefore, that if we cannot overcome conditions, we must adapt ourselves to them. When confronted by a problem or a situation that disturbs our peace of mind, we should meet the situation and eliminate it from our experience. If it is beyond our power to overcome the difficulty, then we must adjust to it. The solution of most of life's problems is a process of adaptation, the conquest of environment. Adjustment begins with what we contribute to experience, not with what we take from it.

If a period of concentrated thinking offers no solution to a difficulty, the average person might begin worrying, as though such a reaction would produce an answer to the problem. The individual begins to fret. Shortly afterward comes the fear of consequences—followed by mental depression, despondency, and brooding. Soon the whole organism is disturbed. Like the emotion of fear, worry directly affects the physiological processes. Strange symptoms result from worry, and immediately the individual begins to attach these symptoms to more serious causes. Worry is a destroyer of health, wealth, love, and expression. Then it creates bigger difficulties to worry about—all the outcome of negative thinking.

Nature did not intend that we should worry. She endowed us with a brain wherein is stored *wisdom, instinct, intellect, willpower, and the power to reason.* Furthermore, Nature intended that we should use these attributes intelligently so that our lives would be such a beautiful, harmonious expression that any condition creating worry would be foreign to our experience.

When we worry, it is generally because we find ourselves in a situation other than that which we anticipated. We did not correctly use our power of wisdom, instinct, intellect, willpower, and reason. In other words, we made a mistake.

We did not have the mental capacity to cope with the situation, or we failed to use our intelligence properly, and we were led into an error. Our plans do not materialize as anticipated, and we find ourselves in an unexpected difficulty.

Then instead of immediately doing something to correct the situation, we just sit down and begin to worry. The mind, being disturbed by the confused state, is then unable to properly govern the body. Consequently, mental and physical trouble develop.

Worry, like fear, will disorganize the whole being—body, mind, and soul. Most people who are ill are the victims of worry. Even if their illness is not a direct outcome of worry, this destructive force is still associated with the condition in some form or degree.

Worry is responsible for more disease than all the germs that exist on the face of the earth. Almost everyone suffers from it in some form or other. Few of us ever realize just what harm we do when we allow our minds to indulge in this most destructive emotion, which has been aptly called the "foolish American pastime."

Findings show that not only do physical conditions create

worry, but that worry itself creates bodily sickness. There is an intimate relationship between high blood pressure, heart failure, and all phases of serious anxiety. Loss of appetite and weight often accompany prolonged worrying. Worry and other destructive emotions and irritations of life hasten the breakdown of the organic functions, and it is well known that emotional disturbances greatly aggravate diseases or deficiencies of these functions.

Worry most often directly causes the various kinds of functional nervous disease. Many people cannot sleep because they worry about their inability to sleep. The more a person concentrates on trying to go to sleep, meanwhile becoming more apprehensive of failure, the more apt that person is to stay awake. The same is true of nervous indigestion. In fact, any part or function of the body is apt to become disordered if too much attention is centered on it. Those bodily processes and functions controlled by the subjective or innate mind are best performed when left undisturbed by orders from the educated mind. This is true of functions other than those that require the most direct and painstaking efforts of conscious attention. In the case of sleep and digestion, for instance, we cannot pay too little attention.

To illustrate exactly how worry in the mind can produce pathology or trouble in the body, consider the following case. John and Sue are a couple in moderate circumstances who wish to enjoy the comforts and conveniences of middle-income life. They decide to purchase a home and furniture. But not having sufficient cash to buy these items, they use credit. They make the purchases—mortgaging their future—and indebt themselves to creditors for years.

The plan works very well for over a year. Then John's

company suffers a downturn and he is laid off. He begins to worry. Sue, who is still working, knows that without both incomes they cannot meet their monthly obligations. She begins to fret and worry. Her mind is being disturbed by this worry, and soon her whole system becomes involved. Sue loses her appetite, her sleep is broken, and she feels depressed and out of sorts. A spirit of gloom settles over the household.

John and Sue decide that they must do something, so they try to borrow some money from the bank. Conditions have changed things, and the bank refuses the loan. Money seems so difficult to raise. They go from place to place and finally are convinced that they cannot get the money. Worry continues, growing in its intensity. There seems no way out.

The collectors call again and again. They threaten to repossess the house, the car, and the furniture. John immediately creates a mental picture of the furniture being moved out. He wonders what the neighbors will say, and this increases his worry. His pride is now involved. He sits and broods all day. Finally he becomes physically ill. (He has already been mentally ill.) His stomach is all out of order and will not retain food. He is nervous and irritable.

Sue comes home and finds John quite ill. She urges him to see a doctor, and he follows her advice. He consults a medical doctor, a chiropractor, and a Christian Science practitioner. Each in turn treats John's physical symptoms without any inquiry into the mental cause of his trouble. John receives some relief from his illness, but the worry that originally made him ill is still there. John continues his quest for a doctor who can successfully cure his malady.

The type of doctor John needs might be difficult to find. It is the same type the entire world needs: *One whose treatment coordinates the body, the mind, and the soul so that all three will work together harmoniously.* To cure John, the doctor must find the real cause—worry—and eliminate it from John's mind, thereby restoring the mind to normal. Then the doctor must treat John's body for the physical condition that the mind caused. When all this has been accomplished, John will be well.

This story illustrates the extent to which worry can affect us. Therefore, it is important that each of us should know and comply with the laws governing worry:

1. Determine the cause of worry.
2. Eliminate the worry through intelligent action.
3. If it is not within our power to intelligently eliminate the worry, then we are to accept the situation as being one over which we have no control, and we are to refuse to worry.
4. We should not create worries. We must plan our acts so intelligently that worries will not develop.

When John and Sue realized that it was no longer possible to pay their bills, John should have used his intelligence and contacted the creditors, honestly explaining the situation. He should have asked that a new arrangement be made, with smaller payments. If the creditors found this unacceptable, John should have realized that it was a situation over which he had no control, and the couple should have allowed the creditors to do what they did in similar conditions. If creditors repossessed the home, the car, and the furniture, the couple should have accepted the situation in a calm, peaceful manner and refused to worry about it. Then they could have adapted themselves to the new situation.

In order to eliminate worry from our experience, we must face life with courage. We must discard biases, as well as the opinions and conventions of others. We cannot be free from the pangs of worry as long as we allow our thinking and our activities to be governed by the beliefs, customs, opinions, and traditions of others—instead of following the guidance and dictates of our true selves.

Living as we do in a world of untruth, the conventions we are called on to observe, if analyzed, seem absurd in many cases. Yet the majority of us are inclined to worry if we cannot fit our lives according to these false standards. The farther we digress from the natural way of life, the greater and more numerous become our anxieties. We must remember the old saying: The standards of man are temporal; those of nature, eternal.

Beyond food, clothing, shelter, health, danger, and the necessities of life, there are no disturbances that rest on the facts themselves. Facts, events, and circumstances take on their color and significance only in the light in which we view them. Everything is relative. There is no big or little, fast or slow, ugly or beautiful, rich or poor—except by comparison. One person feels financially depressed on a certain salary per year; another prospers on the same income. Our outlook is determined and measured by our standards. We judge life not by its realities but by its appearances. Worries are but fantasies of the mind.

In the art of avoiding worry, we must guard against becoming involved in other people's troubles and the conditions they allow to disturb their lives. Unless we build a wall around ourselves, so to speak, intended to protect our peace and happiness, we will be exposed to all of the negative vibrations of people whom we contact. Being subjected to the vibrations of the emotional conflicts of the crowd, we must possess a vigorous constitution to maintain our own emotional stability.

WORRY ⇌ HOPE

Many strive for perfection, and worry about failing to attain those goals. Such individuals lack an understanding of the true principles on which life is built. Every phase of Creation has its imperfections. Life cannot be perfect because it is in the process of evolving and is subject to variation and change. Humanity cannot be without limitations, nor will the products of human effort be flawless. We must make an effort to learn from our failures, losses, and suffering, because through them we grow spiritually: It *is the defeats of life that strengthen us, not the victories.*

Life presents the opportunity for joy and happiness in equal measure with discontent and worry. By understanding the Laws that govern our being we can direct our lives accordingly. Then we can avoid the suffering that results from transgressing these laws and we can avoid the emotional disturbances that come as an inevitable consequence of their violation.

Chapter Seven
SELFISHNESS

Selfishness is the opposite of generosity. It is an offspring of greed and originates in the self-preservation instinct. Selfish people are concerned solely with their own needs, wants, and desires. In the last analysis, selfishness means that a person is living for him or herself alone, unconcerned as to the welfare of others, disinterested in any organization—be it local, state or national.

We are all in love with ourselves to a certain extent. No one wants to change places with anyone else without being assured of personal gratifications. We are all necessarily self-centered. We tend to concentrate on those things that concern us personally and those things that we customarily identify with our real selves. Yet, if all people were selfish, society would be in chaos.

Fortunately, many people have evolved far enough to have eliminated this undesirable trait. Were this not true, governments, organizations, and social gatherings would be impeded by the selfish.

In this world we should recognize that we are on equal footing with our associates. If we should gain the desirable things of life such as wealth, prestige, or fame, we should realize that we acquired them either by chance or by the operation of Natural Law. We should entertain no selfish desire to take away what someone else has rightfully earned.

Many people, due to the operation of Natural Law, acquire riches. Others live in comparative poverty. Those who live in poverty and who do not understand the operation of the Law will be inclined, by comparing their own plight with others, to become selfish to the extent of criticizing, even hating, those more fortunate.

Some individuals have an abundance of the good things of life—more, in fact, than they need. Instead of sharing their excess worldly goods among those less fortunate, they are guilty of ignoring the apparent need of others. Here, again, is an expression of selfishness. If these individuals understood the Natural Law involved, they would comprehend Jesus' teaching: "*It is more blessed to give than to receive.*"

Many an overambitious person who has used selfishness and greed to amass wealth has sought to relieve self-condemnation by engaging in a program of charity and social welfare. Although there is a certain amount of pride and self-satisfaction involved in such philanthropy, still such activities tend to sublimate the baser emotions of greed and selfishness. Even in our homes, where selfishness should find no refuge, many an individual will shower loved ones with gifts on certain occasions to ease the giver's conscience about his or her habitual selfishness.

One of the most difficult lessons we have to learn in life is that we are ONE with all people. Since we are individuals, we are so absorbed in thinking of the self that we tend to ignore the interests of others. Occasionally we need to ponder the fact that the universe must flow out of One Source. It is evident that each of us, being some part of the whole, must share that essence with all others. Therefore, we cannot be completely separated.

One of our greatest mental victories is to comprehend the idea of individuality without separation. Only through such an understanding can we bring help to our friends and neighbors—who are ONE with us in spirit and in essence.

When a person can recognize that all are ONE, that person then becomes altruistic. He or she realizes the truth of the biblical concept: "*Bread cast upon the waters will be returned threefold in time.*" Being familiar with this great spiritual law, such a person gives freely, expecting nothing in return. The Law then compensates him or her threefold.

There was a time in the evolution of human consciousness when selfishness was an asset in self-preservation. But that was the law of prehistoric man. In today's society, selfishness no longer plays a part. It has been outgrown, outmoded, and should be eliminated.

The only effective way to develop ourselves and improve our environment rests on the principle of combination. We as individuals must consciously be aware of, and participate in, the common interests of all other individuals. We must become imbued with a determination to help others succeed that we may succeed—and thus build a common ideal of growth and development. To participate successfully in the lives of others, we cannot at any time selfishly and intentionally deprive others of the things they desire. Nor are we justified in interfering in any way with their growth and development.

To the degree that we assist others to success and happiness, we also increase our abundance and our happiness. As the old saying goes: "*The greatest joy in life is the joy we can give to others.*" It is impossible for us, as fair and reasonable individuals, to believe that we can attain ultimate success by depriving others of what is rightfully theirs. We always find the most complete life when we seek self-expression in integrating all our personal aspirations and desires with those of humanity.

SELFISHNESS ⇌ GENEROSITY

In overcoming selfishness, we must differentiate between egoism on one hand and extreme altruism on the other. If we view all people as actors on the stage of life, we see the slaves of selfishness playing a pathetic role. But no less pathetic is the picture presented by the slaves of mistaken unselfishness. When someone sacrifices at too great an expense of personal welfare, that person is no longer a contributing factor to society. Instead, he or she becomes a burden, actually contributing no more than the slave of greed. Eventually that person breaks down and has to be helped by those whom they hoped to assist. Thus altruism improperly understood causes suffering.

Ironically, the selfish seem to gain ascendancy, for those in whom evil predominates are clever in their schemes and take advantage of the good. Most individuals pervert the innate urge of self-regard by allowing it expression in the destructive force of selfishness. Others, however, in an attempt to escape from the evil of self-love, become the victims of self-neglect.

If, in our attempt to overcome selfishness, we concentrate solely on others and lose all interest in ourselves, then we defeat the purpose we set out to attain, creating a situation that is both unnatural and unethical. Individuals who cease to care for themselves violate the physical, mental, and spiritual laws of their being.

Only those who have developed themselves can be instrumental in assisting others. The real self of someone who attempts to assist another must have such inherent quality that what actions he or she takes for another will help that individual climb upward. All valuable altruism has its roots in a valuable type of person who is being altruistic.

Both a child's behavior and thinking are directed toward the self. The youngster is decidedly egoistic by nature, but the maturely developed and evolved personality is not self-centered. That personality has objective interests and cares about other people. That personality discovers ideals that constitute the guiding principles of his or her life and the lives of others, and is ready to die for them. Such a person is habitually absorbed in creative work and does not evaluate life according to personal possessions and interests. That person's greatest satisfaction comes from projecting life outward, thus finding expression in the benefits of others. As Jesus said, that person "finds life by losing it."

How, then, can the individual span the gap from infantile self-centeredness to this highly developed and evolved maturity? Many adults still live according to a childish pattern. They are censured for being selfish, but if we investigate further we find they are specimens of arrested development.

Only through understanding and obeying the Laws of the Body, Mind, and Soul can the individual span that gap. Just as the body becomes dwarfed through a violation of certain physical laws, so the self is stunted unless it frees itself from the bonds of self-absorption, objectifies itself, discovers itself in family, friends, interests, and loyalties beyond itself.

Along with love and friendship, one of the most enduring satisfactions in life is to lose ourselves in creative work. Every wise person will seek activity in which to find self-expression, an outlet for the higher nature, a task to dignify our days. Deep within every subconscious mind is an innate urge to create, an impulse to construct, an intense desire to express ourselves in a work that becomes an extension of the self. Some of us repress this innate urge. In others, it lies dormant and never reaches the threshold of consciousness. But the history of great personalities shows that whether they were from eminent or humble places, they really expressed themselves. Their common quality is self-expansion and not self-absorption. They found an outlet in objectives not primarily concerned with the self.

Obviously, it would be incorrect to state that all human nature is essentially and altogether selfish. But human nature is so constituted that it does not really blossom until it has been released from the destructive influence of absorbing self-concern. When the innate urge to extend the self reaches its highest expression, we have the world's saviors. Although apparently they seem to be victims of self-sacrifice, they are actually the exponents of exalted self-expansion. Thus the little ego is enlarged and developed into a higher state of being.

But the life of the extended self is not without its trials and tribulations. Those parents who dedicate themselves to the care and protection of their children may be crushed by what happens to them. Someone who devotes their life to a great cause may be shaken by disappointments and failures. All of civilization's progress has been due to the unselfish devotion of those advanced souls who have brought truth to the world.

All truths have been persecuted and vilified by selfish men and women. The histories of great inventions, philosophies and religions verify this. Nevertheless, any wise person with true regard for higher development would choose to face the problems of an expanded personality rather than the dwarfed and narrow life of selfishness.

Reason and wisdom should guide us in coping with life's situations. To give adequately of ourselves or our abundance to a deserving person or cause would be a kind act—provided that such action would not bring suffering to, or impoverish, the giver. But no one is justified in refusing to contribute to a worthy cause or person when such giving does not work a hardship on the donor.

Selfishness is an attribute of the mind that has accompanied human consciousness in its evolution. It has no place on the plane of rational life and should be discarded.

Chapter Eight
VANITY

Whenever the desire for recognition assumes control of our psychic life, it results in a constant striving for power and superiority. This expresses itself in thoughts or activities that seek to display and glorify the self. We soon lose contact with reality, fail to contribute to society or to cooperate with others, and sadly lack a sense of appreciation and understanding of the laws that govern human life. Being primarily concerned with our own reputation and the impression we make on others, our thinking becomes inverted. At this point, our most obvious character trait is vanity.

Vanity is defined as an inordinate desire for the notice, approval, or praise of others. Although vanity is a phase of pride, we may be proud without being vain. But a vain person, ever seeking for approval or commendation, is excessively proud when the desire for personal worth is gratified.

The vain often sacrifice the necessities of life in order to appear well in the eyes of society. They will sacrifice their health and comfort for the sake of being in fashion. They even forfeit peace, love, and security for the sake of wealth and social prestige. Generally speaking, vanity may be described as an extreme stage of self-importance. In this respect its destructive action is at once apparent.

The degree of vanity present, the course of its activities, and the instruments employed to effect its ends, depend entirely on the extent to which we are absorbed and enslaved by this unsocial character trait. No doubt each of us is vain to some degree. But because its external manifestations are generally considered unpleasant, vanity finds expression through the most diverse transformations, concealing and disguising itself at its earliest stage of development.

Vanity clearly indicates that its predominant motive is to conquer everyone and everything. When this tendency begins to dominate our lives, it becomes extremely dangerous. We engage in useless and needless effort centered about the mere pretense of things, ignoring their true nature and value. Our chief concern, then, is the opinions and impressions of others regarding ourselves. We lose an understanding of human relationship, ignore responsibilities in life, and violate the laws that control personal freedom. As a consequence, our outlook on life becomes narrowed and selfish, and we fail in our mission to become a contributing factor to society.

Some people's ambitions are limitless. They ever aspire to achieve something that is considerably beyond their means and capacities. This type of person is discontented unless holding the center of attention. His or her sole object is to outdo another in order to gain personal distinction. An exaggerated ambitious tendency always results from a feeling of inadequacy and inevitably leads the individual to frustration or defeat. The overly ambitious, realizing the futility of their efforts in one line of endeavor, will try another. Thus they go through life attempting everything but accomplishing nothing. In the end they are the victims of disappointment and disillusion. Such people usually lack friends and are difficult to get along with.

Another guise vanity uses to conceal itself is the common trend to be different from others. Some people glory in individuality, in anything that is novel, distinctive, or striking. Their desire to be unusual is reflected in their dress, in their speaking, and in their manners. Their every gesture is directed towards making themselves conspicuous. Many resort to extremes of fashion to attract attention, while others hide their vanity behind the cloak of shabby attire. They make every attempt to camouflage vanity. Close observation, however, reveals that those who are extremely modest, who neglect their appearance, and who adhere to everything old are no less vain than those who go to the opposite extremes.

Another form of vanity is self-admiration or narcissism. Narcissists seek not only for a mirror in which to admire their own physical images but they are overly eager for approval and praise of personal traits and qualities. Any compliment paid to them only accentuates their self-love. Since the vain personality reflects conceit, self-centeredness, and egoism, their character becomes unattractive to others. In the final analysis, narcissists suffer from a loss or lack of the thing that they strive so hard to gain: the love and admiration of others. Those of us fortunate enough to possess personal beauty, health, talents, unusual skill, and capabilities should remember that these gifts are only temporal. They should never inspire self-admiration but only gratitude for their possession while they endure.

Inflated pride and vanity often find expression in posing—attempting to appear greater or pretending to be worthy of commendation rather than striving for it. The pride that some people take in being a "tin god" is often very great. Among the most common types of posing are boasting and flaunting oneself, disparaging oneself, and appearing to be intellectual. Dressing extravagantly and making a showy exhibition of one's possessions are also common ways of posing. People who magnify and make public their accomplishments and who make impressive displays of themselves frequently hope to climb the social ladder.

VANITY ⟨⟩ ASPIRATION

As superficial as appearances are, they are given a place of tremendous importance in human life. That we may appear well before the world forms a major part of human motivations. Society does not ask about the character of its devotee, nor trace antecedents to ascertain their standard of right or wrongdoing. Society only inquires if the person came from a family who has been well stationed politically, intellectually and, above all else, financially. Certainly no blatant crime may be tolerated in the family tree closer than two generations back. But much may be forgiven and forgotten which, on the grounds of decency, would ostracize the individual—if that person didn't carry a polished exterior and a golden mantle thick enough to hide the impurities of his or her nature.

When we speak of society, we do not refer to one class alone but to every class in the whole social fabric. Each has its vanities. Whether these vanities belong to the lowest or to the so-called highest, they operate in exactly the same way. A person free enough from these things to have a bird's-eye view of the whole situation would find it irresistibly ludicrous—were it not so pitifully degrading to the whole human family, and were there not caught in the meshes so many beautiful ones who have lost their way and forgotten their earthly missions.

In every land there are social divisions, whether among the rich or poor, learned or ignorant, or even among the lowest haunts where immorality needs no cover. With all alike, such social divisions are never based on nobility of character but on some vainglorious bauble which humanity has enthroned and tried to inflate with some semblance of reality.

Appearances, however, are not to be altogether despised nor neglected. We should seek to make as good an appearance, according to current standards or individual taste, as can be made without cost to our higher development. If the appearance we wish to make costs justice, honesty, or integrity, then it should be sacrificed. If, on conscientious analysis, we find that our appearance militates for or against personal happiness, then we should sacrifice it until such time as our attitude becomes neutral.

When neutral we may, without danger of vanity, give whatever attention to appearances that the occasion demands. A good appearance without cost to character, genteel manners, and a courteous address born of a kindly nature and regard for others, all tend to soften and harmonize conditions and thus may serve in the path of progression.

The point to emphasize is that it is not our native goodness that makes us valuable in the eyes of the world but, good or evil, how brilliant an appearance we make. Social caste is not based on true merit but on superficial acquirement, whether such acquirement be on the spiritual, intellectual, or physical planes. More and more that requisite is being narrowed down to a mere material acquisition.

It is not uncommon for someone to pose as being intellectual. One popular means of this consists in excessive reference to literature or constantly quoting noted authors to impress the audience with the speaker's familiarity with famous works. Another pretense of possessing a high degree of intelligence and understanding is when someone uses showy or high-sounding language that is unintelligible to the average person. Those whose intellectuality is genuine strive to simplify their diction in order to convey thoughts to others. They use abstract and technical terms only when necessary. It is the mediocre mind that tends to clothe its speech in gaudy and high-sounding terminology.

VANITY ⇌ ASPIRATION

It would be interesting to question an exponent of the caste that has perched itself on the pinnacle of intellectuality and which grows prickly hedges between itself and the "vulgar herd." Tell us, our intellectual friend—you, who have delved into all the ancient and modern lore of the known world—tell us:

- Where do you come from?
- Why are you here?
- What is the purpose of your being?
- Where are you going?
- Do you live after the demise of your body, and if so, what then?

What? YOU do not know these things? We shall give you another trial. Itemize your character. Be honest and analytical in seeing how it measures up.

- Are you self-possessed?
- Do you control your own mind?
- Do you think your own thoughts?
- Do you know whether you think your own thoughts or not?
- Do you get angry?
- Do you criticize or condemn?
- Do you have any ill feeling toward another?
- Is there anyone whom you cannot forgive?
- Are you irritable?
- Do you yield to disturbing influences?
- Are you wide-awake, calm, contented, and happy at all times, under all conditions?
- Are you violating Nature's laws?
- Do you know what Nature's laws are?

If you cannot pass this examination creditably, then take

down your barriers and mingle with common, simple folk. They may teach you some valuable lessons about life and Nature and your responsibility. If your intellectuality has left you wanting in the principles of a self-possessed, noble, pure, and happy life, then, because it assumes so much and gives so little, must it not be classed as vanity of vanities?

Superiority and inferiority are relative. Their presence and contrast are evident in all human experiences and associations. Vanity is always a mark of inferiority. All exaggerated attitudes of superior knowledge, wisdom, authority, and morality are unmistakable indicators of the opposite qualities. They are the most obvious attempts to pose as superiority—weakness masquerading as strength.

We all have at one time experienced a sense of inferiority and therefore desire an appreciable measure of personal pre-eminence and prestige. Thus it is logical to assume that the character and personality of every human being retains a certain degree of vanity. It would be unwise for us to attempt to purge our nature of egoism, self-centeredness, and similar traits as if they were so many demons. Instead, we should recognize the false and destructive nature of those traits and endeavor to redirect such tendencies. We need to divert them into channels of socially useful effort.

As long as the ancestral memories and concepts that profoundly affect our thoughts, feelings, and actions remain buried in the subconscious, they will continue to dominate and control our life and behavior. Once these memories and concepts are brought to the surface and their false nature is exposed, we then begin to take the necessary measures to be liberated from the domination of the lower self.

The extent to which we can free ourselves and find peace

VANITY ⇌ ASPIRATION

depends on our development of willpower and a sense of discrimination. Of all the disruptive tendencies that tend to influence our conscious lives, vanity is one of the first to make its appearance. It is also one of the last to be subdued. Even those of us who have reached an advanced stage of evolutionary progress still show traces of personal vanity.

The vanity and touchiness of so many exponents of our professional fields are marked evidences of a lack of spiritual development. Professional people are still the victims of conceit, egoism, and touchiness which can be attributed to a lack of discrimination regarding true values. Such people tend to overestimate themselves and their abilities. Touchiness associated with any special acquired capacity is due to personal vanity. This vanity originates from an overvaluation of one's specialty and from a lack of discrimination regarding relative values.

It is unwise to be vain about our possessions because they constitute no part of the Divine heritage. Material possessions are temporal, worldly, fleeting. True and lasting happiness comes from within. It finds expression in constructive activity designed to contribute to the larger cooperation of humanity. It is likewise foolish for us to be vain about personal beauty, and it is equally futile to be proud of our financial status or intellectual capacities.

The merit of intellectual capabilities is determined by their social usefulness. If someone is instrumental in promoting the welfare of humanity for all posterity, then the world will pardon his or her vanity as reasonably justified. Discourage all other forms of vanity. They are destructive forces in the life of the individual and of society. Vanity, boastfulness, pride, and self-centeredness are poor tools for acquiring the peace and security essential for happiness.

Chapter Nine
ANGER

He that is slow to anger is better than the mighty; and he that ruleth his spirit than he that taketh a city.—Prov. 16:32

The destructive emotions of the human mind are many, and the individual who understands how to control them is indeed fortunate. Emotion represents a very intimate interaction between the mind and the body. To attain a high degree of self-control, we must begin with the emotions. But instead of suppressing or annihilating them, we should try to control and coordinate them. If left uncontrolled, the emotions eventually evolve into psychic demons that intrude ruthlessly on the confines of the whole being. They create physical and mental disorders, destroying the finer sensibilities, building themselves up into despotic masters, dominating the mind at will and completely supplanting reason and judgment.

Anger may be defined as "a sudden, keen displeasure aroused by real or assumed injury or injustice and usually accompanied by the desire to punish. *Indignation* is intense anger awakened by anything unworthy, as cruelty or meanness; *rage* is a vehement expression of anger; and *fury* is an excess of rage."

Anger, and other similar states, such as rage, fury, vexation, irritation, revenge—and perhaps jealousy and scorn—distort and darken the nature. We should recognize the need to conquer these evils. The human consciousness has become so identified with these destructive emotions that, although we realize these forces are detrimental to our development, we are deluded by the idea that they are a necessary part of human life.

The prevailing belief and tendency is for us to hold the worst in check, preventing these forces from operating where their destructive nature is most pronounced. Such false belief is entirely misleading. We must awaken to the fact that the imperfections retained in our consciousness are detrimental to our well-being—physical, mental, and spiritual. Our progress depends entirely on our efforts to eradicate these animal traits. Until we do, we are not only a slave to the animal elements of our nature but we are subject to all the vibrations around us that arise from similar faults in others.

As we allow ourselves to become more and more involved in character traits brought over from the animal plane of consciousness, we gradually lose our strength of will, our powers of resistance weaken, and our entire organism loses equilibrium. There are some people whose nature is mild and passive, and the expression of anger in such individuals is not so objectionable. Still, this destructive force reaps its penalty and prevents that individual from reaching a higher standard of consciousness. There are others whose natures are intense and aggressive, and the same degree of emotional upset makes such persons most offensive, not only to themselves but to all whom they contact.

The emotion of anger is the perfect example of the striving for power and domination. It reveals very clearly that its objective is to destroy quickly and forcefully any obstruction in the path of its angry victim. Observation and research have taught us that an angry individual will utilize all of his or her powers, physical and mental, to gain superiority and recognition. We often find individuals who respond to the least stimulus that might retard their ambition, or detract from their sense of superiority, with fits of passion, anger, or touchiness.

They are convinced that they can force their issues or conquer their opponents by the use of this weapon. Such persons vibrate on a very low plane, and actually are a menace to society.

There are occasions when anger is justified, but we are considering only the destructive phases of this emotion. Some people actually make a system out of their anger, making themselves conspicuous by their aggressive approach to a problem or situation. They are usually highly sensitive individuals who harbor a false pride. Their inferiority complex is such that they cannot tolerate an equal or a superior, and must themselves be superior to be happy. Consequently, they are ever on the alert lest someone should approach them too closely or fail to treat them with the proper esteem.

One of the most inexcusable forms of lack or loss of self-control is displayed by those who attempt to heal the sick. Too often doctors become irritated and angry at their patients, forgetting for the moment that the patient is ill. Among those who understand the action of the mind, there is a great desire to overlook and excuse the idiosyncrasies of people who live in a state of unrest and illness. It is a flagrant violation of Natural Law to allow ourselves to be dragged down to a lower plane in order to protect an inflated ego.

Often a patient goes to a doctor to seek treatment for some organic disturbance, when in fact the cause is due to emotional upheavals in the patient's life or environment. Treatment of the body alleviates some distress, but no cure can be achieved without correcting the cause. Someone must eradicate the cause—either the doctor with wise advice, or the patient with an awakened understanding. Such cases as these are responsible for some of the failures in healing.

As an illustration of how anger in the mind can produce

pathology in the body, let us assume that a person is eating a meal containing a substance opaque to X-rays. Using a fluoroscope we clearly observe the normal rhythmic churning movements of the stomach. Now, assume that this person becomes angered by a jealous mate's nagging. The peristaltic movements will greatly diminish or may cease altogether. Even milder vexation such as arguments can inhibit stomach movements. Saliva may stop flowing, producing the dry mouth characteristic of rage, fear, or nervous anxiety. Glandular activities of digestion diminish as does the secretion of gastric juice—thus the whole digestive process becomes disordered. Someone who is subject to habitual anger will so weaken the digestive tract that ill health will be the inevitable consequence of this violation of Natural Law.

During fits of anger, every function of the body operates in an extravagant fashion, and all bodily work is performed in a most wasteful manner. All the muscles become tense and contracted. This tenseness pervades even the sympathetic nervous system. As a result, sympathetic discharge creates pronounced circulatory changes. The heart beats more rapidly and with greater amplitude. The smaller blood vessels contract in spasmodic fashion. This constriction of the arteries, together with increased heart action, produces a higher blood pressure and more effective circulation through the organs involved in bodily action. Thus the heart is overworked; the circulation, digestion, and elimination are interfered with; and breathing becomes deeper and more rapid. The entire physical mechanism is disoriented.

Both brain and body perform an enormous amount of work when in a state of anger. However, it is a useless expenditure of vital physical and mental energy—and in addition it does a great deal of harm to both mind and body. People actively

ANGER ⇌ PATIENCE

engaged in systematic and constructive mental and physical endeavors are not apt to become the victims of habitual anger and the harmful, useless, and unwholesome upheavals that result from this most destructive force.

Destructive anger and its associate phases may be listed according to their degree of intensity: irritability, sensitiveness, anger, rage, hatred, and revenge. All are different degrees of the same state—the more intense forms inevitably following in sequence the unrestricted operation of the milder ones. If we are repeatedly detained by mild or subtle weaknesses, our progress is interfered with just as effectively as someone who is subject to the grosser or more intense forms.

Irritability is a subtle form of anger, and the individual who allows him or herself to be affected by it should not be deluded into thinking that indulging in this emotional state will produce no apparent harm. The more intense forms of evil, which eventually take the nature by storm, are simply the more developed states of the milder forms. They exist solely because they were not checked in their incipiency.

The person in whom desire, ambition, selfishness and pride—one or all—are fostered will lose balance and easily become irritated. If unchecked, irritation causes the individual to bristle from points taken in personal offense. When we are conscious of our own worth, we are not easily insulted if accused of, or blamed for, anything that is below our dignity. Most fits of anger or touchiness are simply an expression of insecurity, inferiority, or false pride. Sensitiveness depends on the degree of pride and self-importance that serves as its foundation. If we analyze the consciousness through which we become hurt or offended, we soon recognize that it arises from wounded pride or a sense of self-importance that is not duly appreciated.

When we have risen to the state that tolerates no pride or

special estimation of ourselves, as apart from others, we never take offense at any slight or insult. Our acts are governed by our highest sense of right or duty. We do not allow our judgment to be swayed by the opinion of others, nor do we yield to their influence to any degree.

The thwarted will, directed toward attaining ambition and fulfilling desires, also results in various stages of irritability. The most intense stage is anger. The person with well-developed ambition, pride or indulgence—one or all—will be capable of extreme anger. Anger usually increases to the degree that the will, operating in connection with the above errors, is curtailed.

When we tolerate anger from any cause and allow it to grow, we soon develop hatred that extends to both people and things. Anger against, or hatred of, the most evil condition or person should find no place in anyone who desires health and happiness. We should even check likes and dislikes. Under no circumstances should we allow hatred.

Out of hatred grows the spirit of revenge. Revenge also operates in different degrees, according to the intensity of the force behind it. When we permit a desire or disposition to return evil for evil, or to get even with the wrongdoer, it at once levels us to the plane of our opponent. It feeds the animal natures of both, and poisons the whole organism. The nature of revenge, whether mild or intense, is to wreak vengeance directly on its victims.

When we consider how far the people of the world are from the standard of absolute non-revenge, non-anger, non-hatred or even non-irritability, it is little wonder that injustice almost always accompanies authority. Though we resolve to do right, unless we are free from emotional upsets, the mind is unclear and we cannot form correct judgment at all times.

ANGER ⇌ **PATIENCE**

Everyone needs to learn this lesson, especially those in authority. One class in particular must rid their natures of anger and irritability: teachers, parents, and all who directly control and guide children. Then, not only would children be saved from the polluting influence of such characteristics and resulting injustice, but righteous discipline would be far more effective. The power to control has, in that instance, power to govern others. Anyone who has not gained self-control is, to the degree that he or she lacks it, unfit to be in authority. Progressive individuals support those conditions that provide the greatest usefulness. If someone is angry, hates, or feels vengeful toward any condition or person, that person is thereby unfit to be helpful.

To be forever free from the emotion known as anger means first eliminating its lesser degrees, irritability and sensitiveness. We can do this only by understanding the cause. If the cause is a person, then we must understand that the person is only a victim of destructive emotions and does not understand. We must not allow ourselves to become involved as well. We should strive to develop the art of being patient with people or things that irritate. As a consequence we will enjoy greater health and happiness.

Chapter Ten
DESTRUCTIVE CRITICISM, CONDEMNATION, GOSSIP AND SLANDER

Another scale of errors that plagues the human mind and darkens the soul consists of destructive criticism, condemnation, gossip, and slander. These characteristics are interdependent, and if the milder form is checked, the more virulent phases cannot ensue.

Criticism is an aspect of the mind which, when used in certain ways, is generally considered not only justifiable but exceedingly valuable. Such use of criticism, however, has a limited scope. The original, more restricted meaning of criticism is: *a fine and accurate judgment of an object, especially applied to works of art and literature, with a view of presenting their excellences rather than finding fault.* But usage has caused criticism to degenerate from this standard into an agency for unrestricted faultfinding. As an old saying goes, if those people who carefully pick holes in the character of others would only use the same skill on themselves, nothing could prevent them from breaking through the bonds of ignorance.

Advantageous criticism has very narrow confines. In fact, criticism has become almost wholly destructive. When personal interests are involved, teachers and those in authority may closely scan the work or natures of others directly under their supervision with the sole objective of exposing errors and correcting them. But this is more accurately called analysis, not criticism, according to the way we currently understand and

CRITICISM ⇌ SYMPATHY

use *criticism*. Analysis, used accordingly, divides certain conditions into their various parts to show someone what is destructive and to be avoided and what is constructive and to be cultivated. Only those people who are free from selfish interests should use such analysis—and they should use it only where duty commands.

Critical thoughts—of people, places or things—are definitely negative and constitute the most common form of negative thought. It is a psychological fact that our judgments of others are apt to be self-judgments. We tend to censure and criticize in others the things that are at fault in our own natures. If by criticizing others we could improve our own ways of living and thinking, it might prove beneficial. But when criticism degenerates to undermining others, it can only produce discord and unhappiness in the lives of those who indulge in the pernicious habit. The critical mind forever blames, judges, and condemns the world. Yet little does that critical person contribute toward bettering humanity. Destructive criticism, like jealousy, indicates an inferiority complex; people use criticism to attain superiority over others.

Like all indulged habits, criticism rapidly grows and takes possession of the individual. Then, whatever the surroundings, that individual's peace of mind is marred because of the flaws that present themselves everywhere to his or her fastidious mind. By cultivating the mind according to certain standards, our senses may become so keenly critical that whenever they contact an object, we make comparisons at once and form criticisms corresponding to our likes and dislikes. When any person or thing irritates or annoys us, we should examine our own mind. We will find that we are disturbed through our own criticism. As we cease the criticism, the disturbance passes.

CRITICISM ⇌ SYMPATHY

The habit of using destructive criticism, or faultfinding, stems from a discontented mind. If the faultfinder could regulate the circumstances or people of which he or she complains, it would only vary the state of imperfection. People and conditions of this world can never be changed to satisfy the individual. No two people have the same taste or standards of beauty or desirability. This is a world of endless variety and imperfections, all created according to widely different ideas. If we allow ourselves the privilege of criticizing, even in thought, that which does not conform to our particular fancies, we not only make ourselves and others unnecessarily uncomfortable but we detain our progression toward health and happiness by trifles unworthy of consideration.

It is illogical to conceive of an Infinite Being as imperfect, weak, powerless, poor, indifferent. Yet we allow critical thoughts of the shortcomings and weaknesses of others to color our thinking. God rules the world, plans the world, and must of necessity have different people with varying expressions. We should recognize this fact and be less critical of those with whom we do not vibrate in resonance.

Every individual should strive to acquire the habit of viewing all people as children of God—made in God's image—and to look for such good qualities as are apparent. When we contact an individual who vibrates on a low plane of existence, rather than criticize a weakened or corrupt nature, we should lend our efforts toward directing that person to a better way of life. We must learn to see people, conditions, and things just as they are without being affected by comparisons. By doing so, we soon check the habit of criticism. Whenever we stop justifying firm likes and dislikes, we automatically eliminate critical thoughts and critical speech from our experience.

CRITICISM ⟷ SYMPATHY

Destructive criticism sets off a train of disruptive habits and passions. Because humanity has long given it such free scope, it has become a persistent and insidious habit. Even after the aspirant has conquered other errors and the more obvious aspects of criticism, it often insinuates itself on the unsuspecting mind and once more drags the person into the mire of its own plane. The only way to handle destructive criticism is to throttle it in its incipiency, whenever and wherever it appears.

A critical mind not only checks progression itself, but it leads to the more destructive quality of condemnation. If we do not begin by criticizing, we will not end in condemning. Condemnation is a double-edged sword that very few are capable of using. Indiscriminately handled, as it is today, it is infused with the harmful elements of anger, hatred, and revenge, and is wholly destructive.

Because of the power that evil has gained over humanity, condemnation is occasionally unavoidable. But the circumstances under which it is beneficial are even more limited than those for using criticism. Had humanity not entangled itself in evil, neither criticism nor condemnation would ever have entered human consciousness, much less would it have been necessary to employ either one to promote humanity's advancement. But humanity has become tremendously involved. Therefore it is sometimes indispensable—for someone who is specially appointed—not only to analyze the conditions that hold an individual, but to forcefully denounce them so the individual can also. In extreme cases, when every other method has failed, suffering is the only remaining means of bringing someone to their senses.

When we condemn maliciously, or for any reason except when compelled by duty, we set destructive forces to work within ourselves. We are subject to the law of reaction and open ourselves to disruptive influences that inhabit low planes. Unless we are in a position that unquestionably demands our judgment and regulation, we must never allow our interests to carry us far enough into the affairs or conditions of others to criticize, condemn, or even to form an opinion.

Where indiscriminate criticism and condemnation become habits of mind, it is an easy step to gossip and slander. We will not be discussing slander, for its destructive nature is so thoroughly recognized, it has come under the limit of criminal law.

Gossip, its inevitable forerunner, is considered more innocent. It is, however, both idle and pernicious. We must not allow ourselves to enter any territory except where duty calls. In other words: Strictly mind your own business. If we observe this rule, we will never be led to consider people or things that do not concern us. Gossip is not confined to speaking ill of people, but includes any idle discussion of others' affairs. Anyone who wishes to progress must absolutely cease from any phase or form of gossip.

Gossip is probably the most clearly self-revealing method of personal expression. It extends its destructive forces to the limits of another's possessions, conduct, misfortunes, sufferings, and qualities, and even penetrates the sacred sphere of family ties. The world is full of gossip, and we must closely guard against becoming involved in other people's idle and pernicious chatter. By listening to others' gossip, we become a party to it, and then we are every bit as responsible as those engaged in its actual practice.

Every person possesses both good and bad qualities, and we make the choice to recognize either of these. The prevailing tendency, however, is to ignore others' admirable traits and instead to magnify their shortcomings. But by natural law, whatever measure we use on others will also be used on us. We should closely analyze this statement before indulging in discordant thoughts or idle talk about a person's character or behavior. Gossip is another insidious habit, as difficult to check as it is destructive, and it should be dealt with severely, whenever it interferes.

Criticism, condemnation, gossip, and slander are dangerous forces. Criticism, in the sense of faultfinding, should never enter the thoughts or conduct of anyone who hopes to maintain health, happiness, and peace of mind. Condemnation should be handled only by those who, having gained wisdom, have been specially appointed to authority. Even then it should never be used in malice, anger, irritation or selfishness. Gossip holds the individual on a low plane, and ends in slander—a crime punishable by law.

In a world of imperfections, chaotic conditions, and confusion, it is difficult to remain undisturbed and unaffected by the faults and flaws that are evident everywhere. Human beings have always conceived of the perfect and, because we visualize the perfect but have the imperfect, we are easily inclined to faultfinding and condemnation.

Constructive criticism is desirable and we should encourage it when the occasion demands. But when criticism becomes negative, and therefore destructive, it only contributes to the general chaos of life. We should check this tendency and eliminate it whenever it presents itself. Not until we have risen to the plane where our character is freed from all imperfections are we qualified to censure others.

CRITICISM ⇌ SYMPATHY

Chapter Eleven
ENVY

The trait of envy always accompanies the striving for power and domination. And these tendencies always result from a feeling of inferiority.

If we have an inferior attitude, it shapes and colors our life, exerting a powerful influence over our behavior. Furthermore, such low self-esteem and constant dissatisfaction with life indicate that we have not yet reached a very advanced stage of our evolution. Having acquired a false interpretation of the laws governing the human being, we allow ourselves to be disturbed by the opposites in measuring others' success, their possessions, and personal qualities. Then, we allow others' opinions and accomplishments to guide our decision-making and direct our activities—instead of permitting the Inner Light to illuminate our path. Soon, we become victims of a sense of neglect and feel discriminated against, despite the fact that we may actually be superior to others. These attributes are, indeed, unmistakable evidence of an unsatisfied vanity, of a desire to have more than another person has. As a result, we call the trait of envy into consciousness.

Envy may be defined as *an unpleasant social feeling or attitude aroused in an individual by another's possession or accomplishment of something that the individual lacks or desires.* A feeling of chagrin or resentment is usually associated with envy. Many people's false pride is touched as they see themselves bested in personal qualities or outdone in material possessions. Often the destructive trait will lead an individual into evil ways in order to equal or surpass someone of a superior standing.

Envy finds expression, sometimes, in a person's very countenance. Being an attribute of a low vibratory plane, envy seeks to reduce others to its own level. The envious person, ever wanting superiority, attempts to gain advantage over others in various ways, often by using clever schemes. That person may meet superiors with coolness and indifference, depreciate their qualities or attainments, magnify their weaknesses, or ridicule their aspirations—even seek to retard their progress by placing obstacles in their way. Often someone who entertains an original idea or plan must proceed cautiously to avoid being hindered by an incompetent person who envies others' advancement. Envy may even express itself in the form of personal or material damage to some unfortunate victim.

The feeling of envy that develops in the process of measuring another's success does not contribute to greater happiness. On the contrary, it retards progress by holding its host on a low plane. Attracting as it does those attributes of like destructive character, it can produce only discontent, inharmony, and unhappiness. Despite the universal disapproval of envy due to its socially hostile nature, there is scarcely anyone whose character is entirely free of this trait. As long as our lives move along at the normal speed and momentum, we don't often call the trait of envy into play. But whenever we begin to suffer, when we are deprived of our needs and comforts, when fame, fortune, or love is taken from us—when our present is troubled and our future darkened—then envy assumes control of our consciousness.

Only when we have risen to the state of being no longer enslaved by the opposites—good and bad, wealth and poverty, abundance or lack, fame or obscurity, envy or admiration—when we cease to make comparisons or draw conclusions about others or their possessions, then, and only then, will we cease to desire that which is foreign to our stage of evolutionary development.

Not only must we cease to indulge in envy if we wish to progress mentally and spiritually, but we must refrain from provoking envious tendencies in others. Any ostentatious display of superiority over other people is antagonistic to social well-being. Genuinely superior people conduct themselves in a humble manner and with due respect for those of lesser achievement. They avoid any showy exhibition of their standing that would naturally arouse the chagrin and resentment of those lower in the scale.

Each of us has a part to play in life, and it is our individual duty to fulfill our mission to the best of our ability. We do not always have conscious control over our achievements, or over the nature or extent of our pursuits, successes, or failures. Each individual reacts to life according to their own stage of evolution. Just as it violates mental law to blame, criticize, or condemn someone for their weaknesses, failures, defeats, and wants, we likewise transgress law if we parade or over-emphasize our preeminence, abundance, or superiority.

The saying, "genius is modest," is applicable in overcoming the tendency to incite envy in others because of superior intellectual capabilities. Mental and physical excellences are gifts meant for us to appreciate, enjoy, and use in the interest of individual and social betterment. Anyone who possesses an abundance of material possessions should be moved by generosity toward those less fortunate people who are not as blessed with this world's material goods. Remember, also, the biblical advice: *"charity envieth not, and is not puffed up."* Our achievements, merits, and superior qualities speak through our deeds and require no formal announcement.

The extent to which we long for the possessions or pleasures of another depends on our appreciation of our own environment. The way we view others' wealth, power, and renown depends on our understanding and stage of advancement. If we understand and apply the laws that govern our being, we will welcome others' accomplishments and superior qualities. They become an incentive to strive for better things. If we are sufficiently advanced, our peace of mind will not be disturbed by these things, because then we are too deeply absorbed in constructive thoughts to allow ourselves to become involved in the destructive forces of envy. Anyone who appreciates their own possessions is not inclined to envy.

Many people are unaware of the joys, beauties, and abundance in their immediate surroundings because of their negative attitude. They are always finding fault with their lot in life, comparing their state of affairs with those of a more fortunate nature, anxiously longing for what someone else has instead of utilizing their God-given powers to attain what their hearts desire. Most of our potential powers lie dormant, but if awakened, they could gain for us all that we desire in life. It is our negative thoughts, our fears of lack, of illness, of misfortune, of unhappiness, that actually produce these things in our lives. If we would think health, abundance, contentment, peace and happiness—and lend our efforts in that direction—these things would be added to our experience. As long as we sit back and bemoan our predicament, begrudging others for their better fortune, we will continue to suffer. Only when we recognize that we have the power to use our thoughts to lift ourselves from misery, only then does our freedom begin.

ENVY ⟺ NONINTERFERENCE

Those who allow envy to influence and color their lives are a hindrance to society. Such people constitute a useless, disruptive force that leads toward destructive ends—by disturbing others, depriving them of their rightful possessions, harming them in some form or fashion. Always striving for that which is seemingly beyond their achievement, these people constantly defend their lack of attainment with groundless alibis, usually blaming others for their own failure. Such people are a foreign element in a society where understanding, generosity, cooperation, and love form the bond of human relationships.

Like vanity, the trait of envy claims its victims from the over-ambitious class. Anyone whose aspirations are limited is not as frequently or readily exposed to the forces of envy as someone whose ambitions are boundless. There are some people who cannot enjoy others' accomplishments because they themselves aspire to excel in everything. Everyone has some line of endeavor in which their talent can surpass that of others. But even in their special field, wise people do not strut, or treat those of lesser ability or achievement with disdain.

We would not be human if our personalities did not retain some trace of envy. Since we cannot entirely eliminate envy from our consciousness, we must attempt to control or sublimate it. In the individual, this feeling can be directed toward activities that elevate the person's self-esteem. The same course of action applies to the community and to the nation. Individuals who feel neglected and slighted must be educated in new ways of developing their latent powers, educated in understanding and applying the laws that govern their being. That new knowledge contributes to the individual's own peace and happiness and that of all humanity.

People occupied in a useful activity not only develop personal qualities but often acquire possessions that will diminish their feeling of inferiority. As an individual grows and develops in every phase of being, he or she gains that deeper understanding and broader vision that welcomes the good of others. And that vision eliminates the consciousness of disparity among people.

Let us remember that there is a Power higher than we are that guides and controls human destiny and determines our missions in this life. According to the Divine Plan, everyone is assigned an allotted task to be performed to the best of their ability. Some will be appointed to positions of authority and superiority, while others must serve lower in the scale. But each one constitutes an intricate and essential part in the great scheme of things.

However firmly we may believe that it is within our own power to choose an occupation according to our liking, still there is an Unseen Force that determines who shall be the doctor, the lawyer, the artist, the statesman, the philosopher, the teacher, the servant, the laborer. When we recognize this impelling Force, we should willingly accept our roles and play our parts. Knowing that each part is necessary to the proper functioning of the whole, we will not allow envy to color our attitude toward someone who has been designated to a higher place. The only logical course of action is to accept our own station in life and do our duty to the best of our ability—knowing that it is necessary for our evolution and that in due time we will be elevated to a higher task. It matters not whether someone's calling is exalted or humble, whether king or slave, but only how well the person performs the assigned duties.

Looking at a cross section of human personalities we can see that some are harmonious while others cause constant friction—all designed for each individual's proper advancement along the evolutionary highway. Only when we contact traits of personality that irritate us can we gain a valuable lesson by eliminating similar traits from our own consciousness. Instead of permitting envy to be aroused in our hearts by others' pompous exhibitions, let us rather cope with this destructive force in our own consciousness—and thereby profit from our observation and understanding.

When those about us manifest abundance in the things that we desire for our own lives, let us not envy them, but rather let us be grateful. Their prosperity represents the ever-abundant supply that God has provided for us and of which we may partake according to the degree that we understand and utilize the Law.

Chapter Twelve
GREED

Greed is an excessive desire for power, wealth, luxury, honor, security, prestige, or any personal satisfaction or gratification. Through desire humanity took its first step downward. The desire to gain more knowledge, greater power, and better security—in a shorter time and an easier way than through the process of natural growth—entered the human mind. Thus began the long descent from a state of purity, simplicity, sweetness—and away from possibilities for development that are wholly beyond our present power of conception. The gratification of one desire led to the creation of others, until today humanity is so entangled in the net it has woven about itself that no individual on the earth plane can wholly extricate him or herself.

History has no record of humanity before it began violating laws and, therefore, falling from its native state. We have only the biblical story of the Garden of Eden. The historical record points to ages of wrongdoing, during which humanity has fluctuated through various stages of inferiority. In an effort to compensate for this inferiority, we have the great and complex mechanism called *civilization*. Yet nearly all of civilization would have been practically useless to the exalted and powerful beings into which humanity would have developed, had it not begun transgressing laws and interfering with the natural trend of its being.

All the different historical epochs only define the different stages since the fall of humanity and its long climb up the ladder of artificiality. Humans have invented all kinds of artificial and mechanical means and appliances to overcome the difficulties which beset the way. Those human accomplishments that bolster and patch up our weaknesses we call wonderful progress. Our success is so limited, however, and our infirmities so apparent that we have no choice but to attribute the deficiency to Nature. Thus we lower the standards of human ability, whether mental, physical or spiritual, to the plane appropriate to our action.

If we review human history through the different stages of barbarism and civilization, we find that the differences lie not so much in the moral status of society, nor in the amount of evil that exists, but rather in the crudeness or fineness of the methods pursued. So far as evil's potency is concerned, the differences are in favor of the more primitive states. The civilized human has polished up its exterior and glossed over the reflected ugliness of its savage mind. But that is a sham. Active in the human heart and mind of the present century are all the evils and passions of every known age. While the grosser forms of evil have passed away, we have, step by step, learned to use the human mind to further our selfish ends and to gratify our increasingly complex desires. Thus we have developed an intellect that has taught us the use of finer methods and more subtle forces, placing in our hands greater power to do evil than ever before.

Were it even possible to consider all the past and present phases of earthly conditions, no one could accurately estimate whether, on the whole, evil has increased or decreased during the long ages of its fluctuations. But we can compare humanity's progress with the possibilities of natural growth:

GREED ⇌ **KINDNESS**

- While we have gained in temporal power, we have lost in the real power vested in ourselves.
- While we have gained in intellect and superficial knowledge, we have lost in intelligence and wisdom.
- While we have advanced in mechanical ingenuity, we have lost in the intensity of our senses and brilliance of our faculties.
- While we have found remedies for some of our deficiencies, we have forgotten how to prevent them.
- While we have innumerable ways to gratify our desires, we have lost the key to happiness.

And with all our boasted gains of whatever kind, we have lost consciousness of even the possibility of living up to the standard of a perfected human nature—a standard that is only the first step toward an exalted individuality.

There are thoughts and actions that scatter and destroy the life forces—forces on which the body, mind, and soul feed and depend for health, strength, light, power, wisdom, and even life itself. If we indulge in those thoughts and actions daily and hourly, then no advance in the science of healing, in intellectual accumulation, inventive genius, creations for gratifications, or in artificial practices for spiritual development can keep pace with the destruction we wreak on the very essence of our being.

It is insufficient to comprehend all that is comprised in the Law. It must be as fully lived as comprehended. Neither can we half understand and half live, nor fully understand and partially live. Even though we have fulfilled all the requirements except one, we are not trustworthy, for through that one weakness we may be led into darkness and confusion.

We are always faced with the inflexible Law. We must either stop gratifying our inordinate desires and committing other destructive errors and begin disentangling our fettered being, or else continue in these things and plunge more deeply into the abyss. There is no salvation except by straightening out the distorted nature.

Down through the ages, great teachers have tried to bring the Truth and with it the thought of God's Abundance. But humanity's greed and lust have blinded its vision, and humans have tried to take from one another, instead of cooperating and sharing as is Nature's law. In seeking our individual welfare throughout the ages, we have collectively lost the real issue of supply and demand. As a result, the latter has degenerated to the plane of greed and grasping.

If we cease to use our physical powers, they become inert. Our talents, capacities, and spiritual forces must also find expression, otherwise they will atrophy. We deplete our supply of energy when we fail to use it. Selfish hoarding retards our evolutionary progress, for we are withholding and not using the things that are needed by others. In order to have real value, goodness must be kept in circulation. Someone who shares with others not only practices the virtue of moderation but also shows love and consideration for their neighbor as expressed by the maxim: "Do unto others as you want them to do unto you."

Greed manifests itself not only in the hoarding of material things but also in the inability to give pleasure to another—in an unwillingness to share with a neighbor, or to cooperate in promoting another's welfare. Greedy individuals build walls around themselves to ensure a feeling of security for their wretched possessions.

Greed is closely associated with ambition, vanity, and envy. Inordinate ambition—the grasping for power, the desire to dominate other people—culminates in the formation of a group of complexes that constitute destructive forces in the human mind. Within the limits of this domain, we find the hoarding urge, the saving and accumulating tendencies. Here is where all our greed, selfishness, and covetousness have their origin: the love of material things and the desire to accumulate wealth.

Two thousand years ago the great Master Christ, who was sent by the Divine to give an erring world the Truth, realized that many souls were enslaved by the emotion known as greed. He told humanity, *"Seek ye not these material things which rust and moth will consume, but first seek spiritual things* [or knowledge]; *then all these material things will be added unto you."* Christ realized that people of intelligence would allow material possessions to enslave their souls and pervert their lives. Therefore, He tried to convey the message that these things were false. Seeking material things such as gold, property, power, is purely of the physical plane. These things are temporary, transient, earthly. Due to this understanding, Christ inquired: *"What would it profit you to gain the whole world and lose your own soul?"*

Those who have evolved sufficiently to understand that the entity within, the soul, is the real person, are capable of knowing that treasures, possessions, and powers should have an affinity with the soul instead of with the body. Therefore, they realize that spiritual attributes are more valuable and lasting than all the physical possessions that exist.

There are many people scarcely different from the higher animals who, due to an inordinate ambition, can accumulate vast fortunes. Only the need to maintain self-respect prohibits such individuals from engaging in questionable and dishonest enterprises that may yield them wealth. But someone who has advanced to any extent or degree would not exchange places with such individuals, thereby reverting to their low state of spirituality, even in exchange for all their possessions.

Some people feel so inferior that life would be intolerable for them without the prestige of name, wealth, or power. In such individuals' lives, ambition again becomes the tool of greed and lust. Such expression is a misuse of reason.

The history of the world is strewn with the wrecks of egoistic ambitions. Wars and the fall of nations have resulted from ambitions for aggrandizement. Only when ambition is employed as a socially useful force can it be encouraged. The only constructive outlet for human ambition is to promote a greater knowledge of the world we live in, a better and broader understanding of our neighbors, and a fuller and richer life resulting from the quality of our cooperation. All the other ambitions end in defeat and destruction, or in the tragic crippling of body, mind, and soul.

Until individuals stop considering themselves as entities separate from the Creative Source and also from their neighbors, human society cannot hope to eliminate the elements of savagery and barbarism. Greed and lust will continue to contaminate our homes, our governments, our relationships. Wars and crimes will continue, and humanity will fail to attain the goals to which it aspires.

Our function in life becomes important not as individuals but as parts of the whole. It is in this capacity that humanity becomes "God's greatest revelation." Only by uniting our mental and physical efforts with others can we hope to broaden and elevate our thoughts and experiences, and hence achieve a rational existence.

We should concentrate first on what we can give to life, rather than what we need or can get from it. Too many people approach every situation with the attitude: "What am I getting out of this deal?" To think exclusively in terms of what we must get makes us greedy, selfish, aggressive, egotistical, self-centered. However, thinking in terms of giving makes for humility, generosity, kindness, and cooperation. When we participate in the service of others we receive a greater reward both financially and spiritually. That is because generosity and love, not greed and selfishness, are the fulfillment of the Law on every plane of life—physical, mental, and spiritual. People whose thoughts are centered on giving and doing for others will be amply rewarded by the unfailing Law of Compensation. The person who thinks only of getting, or of getting first and giving afterwards, is deluded by a false interpretation of the Law. Invariably that person ends up with failure and disappointment.

Human history shows that the great artists, thinkers, inventors, and discoverers have been dominated by an inner urge to give the world something that will help humanity—a contribution to all posterity. The creative or constructive thinker does not suppress the creative urge—before even beginning a task—by concentrating on some financial gain or wondering about an eventual reward. Yet, in the final analysis, such a person's reward is greater than anything received by those who do concentrate on material remuneration before applying their talents.

Greed is an offspring of egotism. The opposite of egotism is extreme altruism, which gives everything without due regard for essential personal requirements on the physical plane. Both are wrong in the results they produce.

Wisdom dictates that we should use discretion in providing for basic needs—food, clothing, shelter, essential comforts, recreation. The Great Master made note of this when He said,

"The servant is worthy of his hire." Beyond these essentials, we should have no need to accumulate useless possessions or wealth. We must provide for ourselves in moderation, and we should eliminate any tendency to grab or hoard, to desire beyond our needs and wants, thus limiting the supply that would bless many. The Law of Compensation forever operates and will exact from those who overdraw.

We relate either constructively or destructively to the Creative Power, according to our degree of understanding and ability to control our conscious mind. History is but the story or record of our conscious or unconscious use and direction of this creative force. Those who are ignorant of the Laws of Life have misused this power. Hence greed, lust, envy, wars, and revolutions have surfaced throughout history.

When individual thoughts and ideas unite that are conceived through conscious use of the Creative Principle, it produces an accumulated power. When people are aware of the universal value of such an accumulated power and know, understand, and apply the laws governing their being, there will arise a universal kingdom of peace, harmony, understanding, and cooperation.

When we, as individuals, recognize the truth that all are One, we will know that there can be no happiness, joy, or bliss, in the true sense of the word, until all have attained the highest state of being. Then—and only then—will we realize the great truth of Christ's statement: "It is more blessed to give than to receive."

Chapter Thirteen
DECEIT, HYPOCRISY AND SELF-CONDEMNATION

To thine own self be true, and it shall follow as night the day that thou canst not then be false to any man.–Shakespeare

The part of human nature that is patterned according to Divine law and order is the true self. The form of human thought and expression that is out of harmony with the Divine Plan is the false self. Had the human race not begun wrongdoing, false representation would never have entered the mind. When a spider weaves its web, one strand forms the foundation for another, and every fiber of that intricate little mechanism connects, directly or indirectly, with every other. And the specific purpose of the whole mechanism is to entangle. In this same way, evil has woven the network of perverted human nature, and every individual is caught in it.

The more complex human nature becomes in its errors and the more complete its subjection, the more necessary deception seems–and the more varied its forms become. The further human nature descends from the high state to which it really belongs–*the more it assumes to be what it is not*–the more wicked its means to ends, and the greater its need to cover its tracks. The reasons for deceit and hypocrisy are manifold, depending on the density of the errors in which the individual is involved.

Generally speaking, because people have never been able to forget their ideals, they are unwilling to acknowledge their sins. Individuals represent themselves as being better than they are largely because they lack the courage to judge their own errors. The condemnation of others plays its part, but even if someone does not fear this, their conscience is less troublesome when the evils in their nature are well-cloaked. The exception to this state can be found when someone is sufficiently intelligent to condemn their own errors, whether those errors are known to others or not, for this is the first step to self-purification.

Whenever one person deceives another without just cause, there is an inevitable self-condemnation. We can observe such deceit in all forms of social intercourse. A little child may mislead its parents, but it always suffers the remorse that follows. A student may deceive his superiors and profit temporarily, but in the degree that he or she employs the destructive tool of deception, that student will lose honor and self-respect. Someone may cheat a neighbor and gain momentary advantage, but the price for such transgression must be paid in self-condemnation. Nothing is so destructive as self-condemnation. It causes more misery and suffering than anything inflicted from the outside, because it is a "gnawing pain" deep within our own being. Viewing the past with regret does not help the present nor does it brighten the future. If we repent being involved in some deception, dishonesty, or misrepresentation, the only sensible course of action to follow is to refrain from making the same mistake again.

Doctors of all specialties sometimes resort to a subtle form of deceit because they are not fully aware of the underlying principle of all healing and are conscious of their inadequacy. This is an unavoidable form of deception that can be attributed to the doctor's limited training, for none of the healing

professions is sufficiently broad to embrace the whole phenomena of healing the sick. Many doctors of a high evolutionary status, to escape the self-condemnation of their ignorance,
frequently resort to using drugs or alcohol to escape from consciously realizing they have deceived their patients.

The more someone who is responsible for another's well-
being indulges in deceit or hypocrisy, the greater the penalty
he or she must pay. Sometimes this penalty is a disrupted bodily
condition that results in various forms of illness. It is well known
among psychiatrists that many physiological ills expressing
themselves in the body may be directly traced to a feeling of
guilt caused by deceit and hypocrisy in the mind.

When humanity found that it must either give up its evils or
be exposed, the intellect, which has always ministered to artificial development, gave humans the mantle of misrepresentation. This mantle has been used to its utmost, until today deception and hypocrisy are so universal that their manifold hues
have, consciously and unconsciously, deeply dyed the whole
of human nature. Social relations reek with insincerity and as-
sumption. Religious life has few corners that are not infested
with hypocrisy. Secret disloyalty lurks in home life. Business
life and political life flaunt their prostituted honesty, justice,
and integrity to the four winds of heaven. There is practically
no evil more theoretically condemned and condoned than dishonesty. It is another of greed's hideous offspring, and an in-
separable twin to injustice.

We do not dare effectually attack dishonesty, for such an
attack would reach back to its parentage, whose roots are buried deep in the bowels of civilization. We must tolerate dishonesty, or yield up greed and shake the institutions built on them
from center to circumference.

HYPOCRISY ⇌ **COURAGE**

Suspicion of our own integrity often expresses itself in the constant mistrust of others' honesty. Apprehensive people are uncertain of their own moral integrity. Thus they are ever on the alert in case someone else should be scheming against them. Humanity is predominantly trustworthy, and the confidence that we manifest in other people tends to call forth similar vibrations from them.

It is evident that a person may be honest in certain directions yet suffer deprivations, and it is equally obvious that a person may be dishonest in definite ways yet acquire wealth. If we view the trustworthy person as entirely virtuous and the dishonest one as totally corrupt, we will draw the erroneous conclusion that the one person fails because of particular honesty and the other prospers because of outstanding dishonesty. Closer observation and broader analysis, however, reveal that the honorable person reaps the rewards of upright thoughts and actions but still suffers from the results of vices. Likewise, the dishonest person creates personal misery and happiness in proportion to the evil and the good that he or she projects into life.

It is satisfying to our false nature to believe that suffering can be attributed to our virtue. But not until we have purged every negative thought from our mind and every sinful blemish from our soul, are we in a position to know and to judge that our sufferings are the result of our good and not our bad qualities.

As we progress along the evolutionary path, we will recognize that Divine Law, infinitely just and immutable, forever operates in our mind and life. When we know and understand the laws that govern human life, we will view our past in respect to the time when we were still submerged in darkness, suffering, and confusion. Then we will know that all these past experiences, good and evil, were the inevitable outcome of our evolving self.

In order to arrive at a precisely correct interpretation of good and evil, we must analyze our concepts of right and wrong according to universally accepted standards. If we possess universally accepted concepts of right and wrong, then it follows that good thoughts and actions can never produce bad results and that bad thoughts and actions can never be effective in creating good. Suffering is always the effect of wrong thought in some direction. It is an indication that we are out of harmony with ourselves, with the Law of our being.

It is difficult to pretend to be something we aren't for very long, because after awhile the truth will, by its very nature, reveal itself. Only the self-deluded believe that it is possible to fool others with pretended virtues, appearances, or conduct. No one is deceived except the person who tries to deceive others. Misrepresentation, either direct or implied, to gain our ends or purposes eventually leads to self-degradation, to confusion, suffering, and unhappiness.

Anything that cannot be legitimately gained through developed intelligence and ability must be sacrificed without one moment's hesitation. For anyone who would progress, there is no possible compromise. There must be absolute integrity in every detail of our daily life. Whatever else we are called on to sacrifice, our character must be preserved.

Referring to the more petty forms of deceit and hypocrisy, there is nothing that will add more to our own self-respect, and more quickly demand respect from others, than an unassuming attitude. However little, however humble, *be yourself*. Comparing ourselves with others or emulating them brings destructive forces into play. Therefore we should avoid such thought or activity. Individuality is unique in its expression: No two personalities are identical. Each phase of human expression is as desirable as another, and each is an essential part of a perfect whole.

Among the people we meet daily, there are few whose faces reflect true peace and happiness. Lacking in creative activity, which permits expression of the higher self, and devoid of a knowledge of the laws that govern their being, many people's faces are masked with the artificial, with sensuality, with cold practicality, or with unworthy fears and uncertainty.

To cast aside these masks and attain health, happiness, and peace of mind, we must release ourselves from the sophistication and set patterns of the multitude and follow our truer and less complex personality. We must assemble our inner forces to rid ourselves of our negative identity and return to the actualities of self. To achieve a positive identity, we must refrain from deceit, which will rebound with self-condemnation and throw us into the negative column.

Negativeness in any form eventually produces an instable mind and body. Peace of mind is a far greater possession than any material thing, and we cannot have peace of mind when self-condemnation enters. Eliminating the need to deceive others will ensure greater peace within ourselves and with the world.

HYPOCRISY ⟷ COURAGE

Chapter Fourteen
PREJUDICE AND INTOLERANCE

Prejudice, in the broadest sense, includes all the innate capacities and all the acquired tendencies that create a behavior bias in a human being. In its more restricted sense, however, prejudice may be defined as "premature judgment, bias, often grounded on sentiment, ideas, or associations." The prejudiced mind is a closed mind—narrow, biased, opinionated—one that is inclined to pass judgment before making a full and complete inquiry. In this sense, prejudice is regarded as an evil, an undesirable trait, and it constitutes a retarding force in our evolutionary progress.

We may divide prejudices into two categories—beneficial and destructive. When confronted with an issue in which we must make a decision, we have the right and privilege to investigate all angles and phases of the situation. That procedure indicates precaution and equity and should be encouraged. But if after careful investigation, we find that our prejudice is unjustified, then persistence in our biased attitude constitutes a distinct evil and we should eliminate it from our consciousness.

In the light of prejudice we interpret events and project our fears and hopes onto them. Our distinctive way of thinking and believing influences how we judge or misjudge others. Prejudice forms the eyeglasses through which we view the world and thus molds and shapes both our impressions of the world and our reactions to those impressions.

Whenever someone expresses individuality, a difference of

any kind or manner, prejudice asserts itself. We readily make the false deduction from difference to inferiority or superiority. To the degree that vanity and egoism dominate our behavior, we are inclined to assume that our point of view is the correct one. If others differ, they must be wrong. If they are unlike us, they must be inferior.

Whenever the element of rivalry enters the picture, our prejudice is intensified and often blazes forth in dramatic competition. Wars have always magnified and intensified all sorts of prejudices, making it more difficult to maintain world peace and harmony.

Nearly every person is a crank on some subject or other. Strengthened by conviction and sentiments, mere opinion and belief dominate our thinking, to the extent of obstructing our outlook, clouding our vision, and preventing us from seeing the facts. We dislike following any line of thought or reasoning that is antagonistic to a strong emotional prejudice. The emotional intensity and the quality of the sentiments attached determine the degree to which prejudice can hold and sway the human mind.

All of us have experiences implanted deep in the subconscious memory that help form our opinions and limit our judgment. Too often these experiences would not endure the test of right reason, and the impressions they produce tend to delude and misguide us. Consequently, our minds become confused and imprisoned by prejudices, biases, set opinions, odd ideas and taboos. Without investigating causes and effects, we confidently turn to these subconscious memories for direction in meeting real-life situations. Only when we inquire into experiences and measure effects in the light of their origin can we hope to use experience as a reliable guide.

PREJUDICE ⇄ FORGIVENESS

Our false memories of experiences, submerged in the ignorance-bound regions of the mind, often produce masses of likes and dislikes, ideas of right and wrong, as well as conscience and belief. When called on to answer a question or make a decision about a subject of which we have only limited knowledge, our tendency is to call up such false memories, which then color and sway our thinking. We should instead pursue an unbiased investigation of facts to guide us in making judgments or drawing conclusions.

Prejudice is usually considered an evil, but however much we may disapprove of its existence, we cannot dispense with it. To entirely eliminate prejudice from human experience would require renouncing all convictions, conventions, beliefs, principles, and conscience itself. A principled person maintains an open mind to all issues and does not pass judgment until after making a thorough, unbiased investigation of facts. That person asserts his or her own rights but at the same time respects the rights and privileges of others, permitting them the freedom to think and believe according to their understanding.

By means of prejudice we protect ourselves against unpleasant, undesirable, and thus usually destructive tendencies that militate against our integrity, our peace of mind, our settled convictions. But when prejudice becomes a retarding factor in progress and cooperation, then it is an evil and destroys the very objective it seeks to achieve.

Prejudice leads to intolerance, and intolerance leads to criticism and self-condemnation. Intolerance may be defined as "lack of forbearance, narrow-mindedness with regard to the opinions and beliefs of others; an inability to endure." It is the inability to understand intellectually and to accept emotionally the facts as they are.

PREJUDICE ⇌ FORGIVENESS

We are in the habit of being intolerant. We allow ourselves to be disturbed by the shortcomings and mistakes of others and of ourselves. We concentrate on insignificant details and petty differences. We fail to understand the operation of the Law of Opposites and the Law of Cause and Effect. Intolerance of others leads to criticism. Intolerance of ourselves leads to self-blame and feelings of guilt.

Too often intolerance is not the result of what we think but of how we feel about any particular person, institution, or idea. We are victims of intolerance for as long as we analyze and interpret facts through our emotions. Only through reason do we attain genuine understanding and tolerance. When we feel superior purely on the basis of being born into a particular race, we become intolerant of race, creed, and color. We often boast of tolerance in religion, but in reality question the integrity of anyone of a different faith. How open-minded is someone who concedes that all truth is relative, but who then becomes emotionally upset when someone else expresses ideas that contradict his or her viewpoint?

Yes, we profess that others have the right to solve their problems according to their own dictates, but still we find fault and criticize anyone whose code of behavior is different from our own. As long as we continue feeling tense and irritated by whatever does not conform to our particular desires, notions, or prejudices, we are ignorant of the meaning of tolerance.

It is Spirit's nature to express Itself in many ways and in many forms. If there were no change, no diversity, life would become dull and uninteresting. The Spirit within must, of necessity, express Itself through the medium which It has created. Some media are destined to be on a lower scale than others, and their expression, therefore, is different. And here again the Law of the Opposites is in operation: Without a knowledge of perfection we could not be conscious of imperfection. Therefore, in order to progress we must have both. From these expressions we gain knowledge that enables us to choose— and to progress or retrogress accordingly.

All persons, nations, and races are an integral part of the great scheme of things. Can we say that any race, religious sect, or class of people is inferior and therefore to be despised, mistreated, and cast off? Are we justified in denying them their rights and freedom just because their traditions, standards, customs, and beliefs differ from ours? Why should the color of a person's skin, mode of dress, or religious worship make them the victim of criticism, condemnation, or ridicule? Everyone must express themselves according to their ability and to the limit of their understanding. Therefore, as long as we do not interfere with the welfare of others, who has the right to deny anyone their way of living and thinking? Who has the authority to judge others?

It is only natural and normal that we have individual preferences, but we should not become obsessed with our own ideas and opinions. Everyone is traveling the Path, each seeking their highest good according to their own understanding. No one is perfect. All of us have our limitations. Yet we all struggle onward, and some day each of us in our own way will attain our goal.

What undreamed of heights might we achieve if we would only realize, with understanding, that there is only one mighty Essence permeating all creation? Obedience to the Laws of Life will elevate us to these heights. When enough of us, through obedience to these laws, automatically cease elevating ourselves to the detriment of others, real unity will be assured.

PREJUDICE ⇌ FORGIVENESS

Peace, happiness, and understanding will then prevail throughout the world.

In a progressive world there is no place for intolerance. Humanity is rapidly increasing its storehouse of knowledge. Science is ever discovering new methods of improving our daily lives. Yet if we look at history, we find that the actions of our intolerant ancestors prohibited the world, for a time, from receiving the full benefits of such great inventions as the automobile, the airplane, the steamboat, the telephone. The inventors of these devices were persecuted by the prejudices and intolerances of narrow-minded, biased, critical, and jealous individuals who feared that their security was threatened.

Insecurity is probably the basic reason for our intolerance, as it is for many other destructive attitudes. Nothing is fixed or assured. In our external environment as well as from within ourselves, we are exposed to dangers that challenge our physical, mental, and spiritual security. Every other little security-seeking ego represents a potential danger to our own welfare. Thus we become the victims of fear, jealousy, envy, prejudice, and intolerance—and a score of other evil tendencies. And while we attempt in vain to attain happiness and peace, in our ignorance we destroy it, or at least make it more remote and difficult to attain.

All new systems of thought must undergo a form of crucifixion before being accepted by the world. People blindly cling to their old beliefs, ideas, opinions, and traditions while closing their minds to anything new or different that might contradict or expose some of their convictions. Not only do such people have a closed mind to any new system of thought or religion but they ruthlessly attack, without investigation, anything that might shatter the foundations of their ways of thinking or believing. Remember this saying: *Condemnation without investigation is a mark of ignorance.*

It is wrong to unsettle the minds of those who are not ready to accept the Truth. Only those who are ready will investigate with an open mind and will cast off the mantle of false beliefs, prejudices, and intolerances. Once freed of its old masquerade, the real self, with a broader and deeper understanding, will embark on its crusade onward and upward to a better life.

Chapter Fifteen
JEALOUSY

Characterized by anxiety, envy, distrust, and suspicion, jealousy is an emotional state that manifests itself in the form of a demand for exclusive affection or attention.

Jealousy implies "wounded vanity, conscious or subconscious inferiority, and fear—fear of not being able to hold something desired." It is a character trait that grows out of greed and those conditions that arise from greed. Through perfect accord with Nature's law of action and reaction, greed promotes jealousy, and jealousy increases greed. If greed did not operate in human nature, we would not need to fear that our own, or that which we lawfully acquired, would be taken from us.

Not only does jealousy weaken and disrupt love relationships but it also directs its destructive course into all human ties. We can trace most manifestations of jealousy in adults to some childhood memory or experience in which the feeling of being neglected or the sense of being discriminated against predominated. Jealousy frequently develops in children from a desire for superiority or from fear of being replaced. It is not uncommon to find a child expressing extreme jealousy when a younger brother or sister is introduced into the family, especially when the older child has been the exclusive object of parental love and attention.

Some people's egos are such that they cannot tolerate another person being superior or preferred over them. Thus jealousy is aroused by anyone they cannot equal or surpass. While recognition bestowed on another person is not always deserved, still we can never be justified in indulging in the negative emotion of jealousy. It is a destructive form of hypersensitivity—destructive not so much to its object as to the person who harbors it.

When we have evolved to the point of being conscious of our own faults and limitations, we then react favorably to the recognition of superior qualities in others. When we recognize the ONENESS of all humanity, we realize that an individual's excellence or accomplishment contribute to the betterment of the whole—and therefore to our own personal development as well.

Jealousy assumes various forms and proportions. We can detect it in the destructive criticism of another individual or of that person's accomplishments, in distrust of another or suspicions about that person's activities, and in the fear of being slighted or neglected. The concepts that we have built up in preparation for our social life determine which of these manifestations predominate in us. Jealousy will always express itself in some type of useless opposition—perhaps obstinacy, self-destruction, damaging another's possessions, or in disorganizing someone else's plans and spoiling their pleasures. We may classify the most outstanding—and objectionable—of these manifestations as a restriction of another's freedom. Placing physical, mental, and spiritual bonds around another person only causes the victim to strive to break away from such imprisonment.

Jealousy is generally considered to be an inborn tendency, but even a superficial glance at its effects contradicts that erroneous conclusion. Instead, this aggressive force is a logical and rational tool, unconsciously acquired in order to enslave another human being. Jealousy is the unfailing index of an inferiority complex. It is an artificially prepared emotional feeling that exerts its harmful influence both on the jealous individual and on the unfortunate object of this destructive trait. In terms of its destructiveness to the whole being, we can compare jealousy to hatred, its close relative. That great love is impossible without some jealousy is a tragic fallacy that prevails in most people's minds.

Whenever we are jealous, we tacitly acknowledge our inability to maintain the love of a beloved and further admit our unworthiness of that affection. Therefore, we resort to the artificial limits and restrictions of jealousy to avoid any outside competition that might reflect on our own inferior status. When we attempt to command and own those we love through bonds of jealousy, we deny our loved ones the freedom of thought and activity indispensable to preserving enduring love.

The very nature of jealousy condemns it, and only in an abnormal life can it find expression. Its nature is revealed through its action: to clutch, grasp, and bind for personal gratification.

It also gives rise to suspicion, hatred, and anger. It pollutes the nature in which it exists and poisons the atmosphere breathed by its victims. There is no circumstance or relationship that justifies its presence, yet people are deluded by the idea that it is supposed to accompany love. Be assured that where jealousy exists, REAL LOVE IS UNKNOWN. In its place is only an unholy emotion born of lust for self. Jealousy is like a poison ivy that grows around the tree of love, choking its branches and withering its roots.

Jealousy is not an attractive force but a repellent one. Those who become jealous of another's love or attention take the very attitude most detrimental to their desire. The desire is in no sense justifiable, but from a selfish standpoint, jealousy dramatically opposes the ability to achieve their goals. A victim of jealousy naturally resists the unjust bondage to which such jealousy subjects him or her. Therefore, the more intensely we clutch at someone, the greater they resist and the wider the breach becomes.

UNSELFISH LOVE is the attractive force. When this is not active or when it is not enough to unite and harmonize, all efforts on low planes become useless. We may watch and guard our possessions as we will, but we will never be able to ensure them against the destructive forces that operate everywhere on the same low plane as jealousy. This state is as useless as it is destructive.

If we imagine that our happiness depends on a person, place, condition, or circumstance—thus becoming jealous—we are pitifully deluded. Happiness is born of a pure spirit. The more absorbing our jealousy becomes, the more miserable our plight. So again our end is defeated. Jealous thoughts upset the entire organism—body, mind, and soul—and bring on a nervous condition that all the doctors in the world cannot cure.

If we are inclined to be jealous of other people or things, we can be sure that deep in our subjective mind are concepts from past experiences of childhood days, acquired from a misuse of reason at that time. These concepts activate at the most inopportune moments and enslave us. Through understanding mental laws, we can closely analyze our jealousies. Realizing that such emotional states are destructive to our health and happiness, we will strive to eliminate them through intelligent thought.

Let us cease to be jealous, for happiness comes from within—never from without—and it depends on no person, place, or thing.

Chapter Sixteen
HATRED

All human life is in a state of constant change and evolution. Some individuals still vibrate on a very low plane of existence—physically, mentally, and spiritually. Others have advanced to a highly developed stage. In the lower depths, life is shrouded in ignorance, discord, and gloom, while at the higher levels it abounds in wisdom, love, peace and harmony.

The expression of life always takes on the values of its plane of evolution. Those who are still submerged are imprisoned by ignorance and indolence and governed by fear, doubt, worry, hatred, jealousy, greed, and all the other negative attributes that keep us in darkness and confusion. There is little difference between the animal with its lack of reason and the person with a limited degree of intelligence and discrimination. As long as an individual's heart harbors the destructive emotions that color the life and behavior of the animal and the savage, there is little hope for that person's advancement.

Once these negative tendencies have gained weight and momentum in someone's personality, they will wreak destruction and disaster throughout his or her experience, finally resulting in mental bitterness, physical disease, and spiritual disintegration. Ignorance of mental laws permits these forces to govern and control our lives. Among the most destructive of these forces is the emotion of hatred.

The Spirit within ever strives to break through the barrier of ignorance and direct the soul to a better way of life. When this barrier is penetrated, we feel a revulsion against savagery and

HATRED ⇌ LOVE

animalism, and we begin to climb upward. At that moment the stream of materialism gradually loses its power to absorb us, and our character expressions manifest less and less of the animal traits.

Whatever the mind firmly believes in and adheres to tends to shape and mold the thought patterns that find outward expression in our personality, character, and conduct. Once these inner concepts are changed, our whole life and experience takes on a different form and expression. Those who master their animal nature and rise above it find themselves in and of a new world.

If we draw a horizontal line and call it the relationship of personalities, we would place LOVE—the highest attribute of the human soul—at one end. At the other end we would place its opposite, HATRED. Every thought, act, or expression between personalities must, of necessity, find its resting place somewhere along this line. Hatred is the negative aspect of what we call love. It can be described as *an emotional attitude characterized by anger and an extreme aversion, enmity, and ill-will, together with a desire to inflict injury upon some individual or object.* Actually, hatred is an associate state of anger, the action of which has already been discussed in a previous chapter.

Let us go back in imagination along the evolutionary highway to the time when the first spark of reason was given to the soul. We might then observe one of the first crude manifestations of human life walking through the woods and experiencing a terrific storm. The roar of thunder and crash of lightning are incomprehensible to that human. As it looks up in wonderment, its reaction is fear—the same reaction we have today to things we do not understand. At that point, terrible fear takes possession of the consciousness. It is a mental law that whatever the mind does not understand, it will either fear or worship. When something that arouses the emotional state of fear does not inspire awe, admiration, or worship, it provokes hostility, a form of hatred.

Hatred, therefore, is an aspect of fear. We hate our enemies because we fear them. We scorn those whom we do not fear. Where there is no fear, there is no hate. Despite all the chaos, destruction, and suffering rampant in the world today, there are many who still remain calm and poised in their thinking. Their hearts are not filled with hatred, for they are confident that good will ultimately prevail.

Few of us are conscious of the fact that great conflicts among nations have their origin in the hatred and greed nourished in individual minds. One of the most disastrous beliefs of the great majority of people is that they are justified in their hate. But not until our individual minds are purged of hatred, greed—and all their attending evils—will there be hope for an enduring peace. The wars of the world will not cease forever until humanity learns and applies the lessons of the Great Teacher who urged that we should *love those who hate us*—that we must fill our hearts so full of love there is no room for hate.

The concept of hatred born in prehistoric humans has been transmitted to their descendants as part of their heritage. The little child, having inherited from its ancestors all the accumulation of destructive emotions, is very easily led into error. With the proper guidance and under normal environmental conditions, however, the child gradually learns to recognize those objects that are conducive to its well-being and therefore to be desired and loved. It also recognizes those that are destructive to its progress and therefore to be feared, avoided, or fought against. As soon as the child acquires the power to make careful and accurate distinctions, the aggressive or destructive tendencies will find an outlet in constructive channels, thus promoting the individual's welfare.

As the modern child is thwarted in expressing natural tendencies and unsocial habits, it is denied the love that is necessary to compensate for its sacrifices. It is no surprise, therefore, that the average child grows up with a lack of the affection required to nurture its *love concepts*. A certain amount of restriction must be imposed on a child's conduct, but when these limitations are accompanied by the parents' expression of hostility toward a child because it intrudes upon their time, comfort, or pleasure, it is little wonder that such children become embittered and suffer from repression.

Hatred does not always appear openly but, like vanity, knows how to mask itself. It often appears in the guise of parental love and guidance. Some parents expose their children to the same harsh treatment and sufferings that they had to endure as youngsters. Deluded by the idea that they are rearing their children according to "good old-fashioned principles," they are actually impressing their children's subconscious minds with the same concepts of hatred and revenge that are so clearly displayed in their own disciplinary measures. Children soon recognize such hypocrisy and that their parents are able to dominate them only because of their superior strength and size. Such children grow up desiring to reach adulthood so that they can assert authority and power through punishment and restriction of those who are weaker than they are. Thus the revenge of parent upon child is perpetuated for another generation.

Parents, guardians, and teachers impose innumerable injustices on children. Some parents and superiors are harsh, inconsistent, threatening, unreasonable, jealous, and even quarrelsome with those entrusted to their care. They burden a child with their own worries, problems, and anxieties, and often criticize and embarrass the child, exposing his or her weaknesses and shortcomings. Yet in return they demand the child's love and respect.

Absorbing a child's personality and unreasonably limiting its freedom can bring only physical, mental, and spiritual suffering to both child and parent. No one can love superiors who hold them in bondage. If we could provide children with an atmosphere of affection and understanding instead of one colored by restriction, compulsion, and violence, the emotional balance of the younger generation would be assured so that their subsequent lives would be freer from the aggressive tendencies that tend to destroy their health and happiness.

To cope with the hatreds and enmities that accompany adult life, we must recognize their origin and background in childhood experience. Most parents are unconscious of the injuries they inflict on their children who, in turn, repress the memories of these experiences into unconsciousness so that they too become unaware of them. Most of us have passed through childhood and are now combating the hostilities that present themselves in the outside world. Yet at the same time we must battle the conflicts within our own personalities that give rise to uncontrolled hatred.

What course of action, then, must we follow to better human relationship? What methods are effective in cultivating love and in controlling or diminishing hatred? A knowledge of and obedience to the laws that govern human life give us the answers to these questions. By understanding the truth, we shall cease to frustrate each other. The basis for peace and harmony in the home, the community, the nation, and among nations, rests on correctly understanding human nature.

In each of us, there is a spark of Divinity. As long as we are disturbed by hatreds and misunderstandings, we tend to disintegrate our consciousness. Harmony and love must originate from within our own consciousness. Any thought or feeling that tends to create inner conflict must be eliminated.

We cannot achieve this end by excluding irritating personalities from our experience, by avoiding or pushing them aside. We must face them and attempt to teach them the laws that govern human conduct. We must strive to redirect their aggressive tendencies and reshape their lives through love, kindness, and understanding. We must radiate so much love toward the annoying personality until no pain, jealousy, resentment or bitterness remains. Only when we dissolve confusion, hatred, and resentment are we at peace with ourselves and with others.

All hatred is dangerous. It blinds and darkens the soul, poisons the mind, and brings suffering to the body. One who has progressed sufficiently to know that there are natural laws governing human conduct soon recognizes that the immutable Law of Cause and Effect forever operates. This law exacts from everyone precisely what is due, for *as you sow, so shall you reap.* As long as we plant seeds of hatred, resentment, and revenge, only bitterness and suffering will be our yield.

If another person has harmed us and we feel justified in hating him or her, let us first analyze the situation. We will recognize that it is the animal traits displayed and not the individual that we despise. If we would just penetrate beneath the surface, we would find the same God Power within the offensive person that is present in everyone. The only difference is that such an individual is still enslaved by their animal nature.

HATRED ⇌ LOVE

Let us not stoop to their low plane by retaliating with like destructive traits, but rather let us seek to show them—through love and understanding—the lighted path. Remember that the penalty for hatred is hate with all its accompanying evils. And the reward for love is love with all its ennobling attributes.

Part Three

THE LAWS OF THE SOUL

Chapter Seventeen
FAITH

Christ recognized faith as a great attribute of the human soul. Being aware of its power and magnitude, he said: "*If ye have faith as a grain of mustard seed, ye shall say unto this mountain, 'Remove hence to yonder place,' and it shall remove and nothing shall be impossible to you.*" (Matt. 17:20)

Endowed with faith, humanity has magnified its strength, courage, and power. Humanity's greatness has been displayed by obscure individuals who have had faith in an idea or an ideal. Faith is the great, inspiring and buoyant force that tides us over the difficulties of life, the uncertainties, disappointments, and failures that tend to obstruct the path of progression. Whenever a powerful, one-directional drive takes possession of someone's life, it can always be traced to faith in or knowledge of a vision, a plan, another person or persons.

Faith means confidence in the integrity of the natural world order, in the infallibility of law, and in uniformity among the facts of cause and effect. It is an abiding trust that all is well because life is governed and protected by Superlative Powers which do not fail.

In the beginning humanity knew the powers that governed and protected individual lives. Everyone knew the laws of Nature and their unfailing results. So long as people were simple and obedient, all activities aligned with a perfect confidence that life was governed to promote humanity's highest well-being.

Through personal indiscretions, humanity began to transgress the laws of being. As its nature became darkened, the light that was still able to penetrate the errors took on the coloring of those increasing impurities, and their operations and results became correspondingly mixed. Opposites of good and evil were born in this state, and the long conflict began. One of the first costs that erring humanity paid was the sweet, peace-preserving faith in the happy fruition of life and its activities.

Faith on the physical plane is prompted and controlled almost entirely by organic forces that are, for the most part, unconscious. But human beings, endowed with reason and the power of abstract thought, employ faith as a substitute for exact knowledge in our efforts to interpret the meaning and value of life. We penetrate beneath the surface of things, looking beyond the facts of immediate experience. In the absence of tangible evidence, faith must supply the inspiration and courage to go ahead.

When we center our intelligence on objectives we desire to achieve, such intellectual endeavor is always inspired by faith in something. In scientific investigations and in philosophical thought, we must rely on faith to provide the realities not present in consciousness. We must always accept unknown factors or qualities on faith to complete the solution, the structure, the design.

In the healing realm are many and varied systems, but all of them depend on faith for their effectiveness. Even Christ, the Great Healer, recognized that faith was a necessary requisite to cure.

Faith is the master key to great discovery, invention, and achievement. Faith is not blind, artificial, or credulous—nor is it synonymous with ordinary belief. Belief is of the intellect, but faith is of the soul.

There is a saying that no person is the whole of him or herself; those to whom we give our faith are the rest of us. When we transcend the limits of our being and reach out to others whom we understand and sincerely believe in—incorporating and blending our lives with theirs—then our lives become transformed, empowered, and enriched.

Only by believing in others do our personalities reach their fullest and highest state of development. In all human contacts and relationships, faith is the keynote of success. In the home, the community, the nation, and the world at large, faith in the people concerned is indispensable in securing lasting harmony, understanding, peace, and happiness.

We cannot find real happiness in love that does not also encompass faith. Romantic love may constitute the nature and basis of many a home, but the substance of faith is essential in assuring its permanency. Without this abiding trust, the home is but a dwelling place built on the foundations of shifting sands. Faith is the bond that perpetuates human understanding and friendship.

All thoughts strive for outward bodily expression. Thoughts of health are vastly more important than thoughts of illness, for to the degree that thoughts are positive they will materialize themselves in the body as health. So the manner in which we handle our faith-function is vitally important, even to physical health. We can no longer separate the physical and the psychic in the diagnosis and treatment of disease. The whole person is involved in illness—and its cure. Therefore, the importance of a constructive use of the faith-function cannot be overemphasized.

Where there is no faith there is no cure, unless the illness is caused by a purely physical medium. Whenever the psychic is involved, as in the great majority of illnesses, faith is imperative. Miracles of healing always result when the one to be healed comes into harmony with the Divine by applying physical, mental, and spiritual laws.

Viewed in this light, we can no longer regard miracles as supernatural. If the whole being—body, mind and soul—is master over fear, anxiety, hatred, resentment, jealousy, selfishness, we automatically bring ourselves in harmony with a great part of Divine Law. Consequently, we become strengthened, physically, mentally, and spiritually.

When we lose faith in life in general, we can be compared to a boat without a rudder, tossed about on the waves of life. This condition is not conducive to health and happiness. Mental and spiritual dissatisfaction often results when we lack faith in the wholeness of life. This brings so much bitterness and confusion that it causes physical inharmonies. We can trace many physical diseases to this cause.

Nothing is more effective in bracing a shattered or broken life than positive faith. However futile, useless, or deplorable a situation may appear, faith will buoy up our spirits. This is especially true with genuine religious faith. Although the faith-function is often exposed to grave misuse in the religious realm, confident faith is still the only salvation for many insecure and shaken lives. Such people will never find solace, coherence, and peace of mind without it.

People today seek and long for a method of harmonizing with the Divine within. Religion satisfies some people. A great majority of us, however, are seekers. Somewhere along life's highway we may find a system of thought or of philosophy that gives us that priceless attribute of faith. Only when we find the Truth, or True Knowledge, do we no longer need faith to satisfy our seeking soul. Only by understanding and obeying the laws governing the body, mind, and soul can we hope to realize any real emancipation from illness, negative thought, and limitation.

Often when a crisis occurs in our life we discover that our held beliefs are not our real beliefs at all. We become aware that beneath this superficial creedalism is our true attitude toward, and concept of, life. This is our real faith—a complete view of the meaning of life in this universe, a powerful force that must find expression in shaping our character and personality. One of life's tragedies is when a person has nothing tangible to place faith in. That person becomes neurotic, ill, discontented and fearful. Life then has no plan, and therefore no meaning. To such an individual, faith in something or someone revitalizes the whole being—body, mind, and soul.

Many people claim to feel a quality called *faith in God*. This abstract idea is based on widely divergent theories that have accumulated as humanity has passed through the different stages of intellectual development. If faith is not born of a clear understanding of unvarying and irrefutable truths, it degenerates into a pretense or counterfeit emotion set on a foundation of shifting beliefs.

To gain the truth underlying all these inherited and acquired beliefs, we must analyze them thoroughly. We all have our own interpretation of life's basic meaning. We obtained this idea through our environment and by association with persons and things. When we apply the light of truth, we can easily discard the false ideas.

The idea that faith is associated only with our religious experience results from incorrect reasoning. Faith is a faculty of the soul that finds its most perfect expression in the spiritual nature. But it must be developed in all of its phases to manifest its complete character. Spiritual understanding does not imply anything strange, unnatural, or incomprehensible. But it does mean that our belief in goodness must be the supreme master over any apparent manifestation of evil.

We must have faith in the Laws of the Soul if through their operation we hope to mold our characters and shape our personalities. Success in life depends on the faith we have in others, while the goal of achievement that we have set for ourselves is anchored in the faith we have in our own ability. We must have faith in the beneficence of Law as applied to life, for the Source of all Law is the Omnipotent God.

Faith is an inherent attribute of the human soul. As the soul has evolved throughout all the past ages, it has retained the essence of the memories of its past lives and knows by experience that in each crisis God always comes to its aid. From this experience we draw the priceless attribute of faith—faith in the eternal, upward progression of life.

When crises come into human affairs—as a necessary part of cosmic evolution—our minds become confused. The confusion leads to discord and fear. People see the old order being swept away and view the future with bewilderment. But, as in the past, God always prepares someone who has been selected and trained. When the stage has been set, that person assumes and plays the destined role.

Two thousand years ago such a crisis came upon the earth. Rome was in her glory; she dreamed of philosophy and dominions without end. But a new age dawned with the birth of Christ. He ministered in Palestine and taught the new philosophy of life. Men of that day didn't know that His message gave birth to a new species of thought, but after two thousand years have elapsed, we of this generation can see that His message was, indeed, the end of an era.

There is a similar crisis today, and not one nation but all nations are involved. The world is confused and afraid. Everywhere people look for a teacher. Where is the person whom God has selected, whose mind holds the remedy for the world's ills? In whose heart is the spirit and in whose hand lies the power to alleviate the sufferings of the world? From the hearts of people the world over a cry has gone forth for a teacher, and from the bosom of God that teacher shall come. The world awaits.

What will that person's mission be? What could it be but to carry the work of the Spirit one step further. The day has passed when humanity can go forward with greed as a criterion. This new age being ushered in demands that we be Children of God in deed and not merely in name. Until this teacher comes, this new age will drag slowly along. When the great destined personality arrives upon the earth, whatever that person says, teaches, and does will prove that person to be the Chosen One.

Then, due to the new teaching, science will be our religion and religion our art. We will cease to be slaves of unknown forces. Then we will know that this universe and all life is ordained by beneficent Law—that our bodies, minds, and souls are governed by Law—and only through obedience to these Laws shall we assume our heritage.

Those who obey the Law will know Divinity within; those who transgress it will again descend into the abyss from which they came. Again and again they will come to rebirth until finally they learn the lesson of life. Until that hour the Spirit toils at its hidden work. Through the hidden light, the Spirit reveals to advanced souls its process of evolution while shaping from out of the dust the immortal Children of God.

Christ foretold that the time would come when the knowledge of God's Laws would cover the earth. The Prophet was right. People are losing faith in the philosophies that embody superstitions and fears, and are beginning to understand that this is a universe of law and order. Jesus declared many times that faith was essential for the many remarkable healings of his ministry. The secret of this teaching is that faith was needed in the absence of perfect knowledge of the laws involved.

Faith is necessary when we possess limited knowledge in the thing in which we have faith. But when we obtain perfect knowledge of that thing, faith is no longer needed. Faith is the great transforming power of all life and brings in its wake the Divine inheritances of health, happiness, and the more abundant life.

Chapter Eighteen
HOPE

God endowed the first single cell of life, and therefore the latent soul, with the capacity to acquire attributes necessary for it to struggle upward from the planes of darkness to the planes of light and become an individualized, fully-awakened human soul. Incarnated as it was in its many multiple forms, it experienced certain stages of evolution, many of which led to despair and gloom. The latent soul at first was devoid of hope. Being exposed, however, to repeated calamities that apparently were fatal, the soul surprisingly survived these crises. Thus hope originated as an inherent capacity of the human soul.

Through the long, dark ages of the past, the soul gained the knowledge that even though its material form was dissolved by death, it remained secure and possessed the accumulated knowledge of all the errors of its past lives. This experience naturally led the soul to believe that it could climb upward regardless of its apparent material position at any given time. Therefore, each human soul has an attribute, based upon experience, called *hope*—hope in the upward progression of life.

Each of us is dual. We possess a carnal consciousness, which is the result of all experiences since birth. We also possess a spiritual consciousness, which is the accumulation of all experiences since creation. Unfortunately, most of us are only aware of the material consciousness, but working within ourselves is this great spiritual consciousness that possesses all knowledge. The whole purpose of the soul's evolution is that it may eventually become cognizant of its Divine origin. Through acquir-

HOPE ⇌ **WORRY**

ing wisdom, the soul can then bring itself into harmony with God, its Source. Obedience to the Laws governing the body, mind, and soul enables the carnal consciousness to work in harmony with, instead of contrary to, the spiritual consciousness. Toward this end we toil.

The carnal consciousness, with limited experience, finds itself confronted with an unsolvable situation. When it sees no way out, it frequently gives up to what is known as despair. Life becomes dark, undesirable, meaningless. Were it not for the indispensable emotion of hope, which lies dormant in each human soul, this particular carnal consciousness would eliminate itself through self-destruction. But always the voice of past experience comes to the rescue saying, "Have hope."

Even doctors, when confronted with a disease that they know will prove fatal to the patient, will bring encouragement with the words, "Where there is life, there is hope." And this hope rests upon the fact that each soul has within itself the accumulated memories of past lives and knows that it is indestructible.

Temporarily the human consciousness may conclude that the body is the entire person, and viewing the dissolution of the body by disease, it believes that all is lost and that death will be the inevitable result. Still the invincible spirit of hope clamors for acknowledgment. Then that person calls on those in whom he or she has faith to intervene. The individual called may be a doctor, a religious figure, or another person, but that act is always an expression of hope.

The human soul, having its memory of the past unavailable to the carnal consciousness, can never be without hope. During the dark, dismal ages of the past it experienced trials and tribulations never known in this material life. Having always survived the expected annihilation, the soul knows it is immune to lesser destructive forces.

To this knowledge we can attribute the spirit known as hope—hope in the immortal evolution of life. During the evolution of the human soul from the first stage of life to its present form, there has been a gradual acquisition of knowledge that enables the human soul to become aware of its divinity and immortality.

Immortality is our supreme hope and constitutes the greatest venture of faith. The hope of life after death provides an incentive for moral perfection. It enlarges and intensifies the worth of personality. It gives significance to many facts of human experience that would otherwise be meaningless. On this hope rests our faith in the inherent beneficence of the world order, our discrimination of values, and our conviction that truth and justice will ultimately prevail. The hope of immortality constitutes one of the greatest stabilizing forces for all humanity.

As the soul evolves and becomes conscious of its destiny, it begins to differentiate between the true and the false. It realizes that some individuals personify the attributes of good, while others are an expression of evil. With its gift of reason and choice, the soul affiliates itself with one or the other. If it aligns itself with those who are good, it becomes, in a sense, the agent of the Divine. By its acts it assists in bringing to a realization the unity of all humanity. But, on the other hand, if it affiliates with the exponents of evil, it increases their power. Thus life moves on, either positive or negative.

When negative elements predominate in human life, God decrees that justice shall prevail and sends someone who can, through teaching and example, remind the human mind of the realities that exist, thereby creating order out of chaos. Due to this Divine action, the human soul, which has experienced these

HOPE ⟷ WORRY

things in the past, is imbued with the spirit of hope.

Anyone who is ill, has problems, and who despairs should heed the old saying, "God's in His heaven, all's right with the world." Nothing happens by chance. All is according to a Divine Plan. That which causes an individual despair has been sent so that the individual may overcome the obstacle and advance upward in the eternal progression of life.

Were it not for the survival of hope, in many instances, by the time a person had suffered enough to be willing and obedient to the laws that operate for humanity's good, that person would have no incentive for effort. In fact, hope is the motive power of all effort. It is the attribute that becomes the stepping-stone to the soul's awakening. Out of the awakening inevitably grows an abiding faith in the powers that operate through Nature to bless the pure life and lead humanity along the path of unbroken progression to higher and higher states of nobility and happiness.

There are two kinds of hope. One is hope in the eternal progression of life and all its goodness. The other is the perverted idea of life for material gain. The first is purely spiritual, born of a desire to serve the masses. The second seeks personal gain. In that instance, hope is largely centered in things that have only temporal value—and even in the gratification of desires and selfishness. Still the very nature of hope, especially its persistence, lends humanity a buoyancy that aids it from sinking into greater darkness and despair. For someone who lives on the plane of desire, hope must survive the person's dissatisfaction with repeated disappointment and failure—or satiation through gratification—until that soul is led, step by step, to see that the ultimate of all hope lies in purity, simplicity, and obedience to Nature.

Chapter Nineteen
GENEROSITY - CHARITY

And though I have the gift of prophecy, and understand all mysteries, and all knowledge; and though I have all faith, so that I could remove mountains, and have not charity, I am nothing.—I Cor. 13:2

Great fallacies prevail regarding the nature and significance of true charity, or generosity. Much so-called "charity" is done through a sense of obligation and not as an expression of love. The majority of people feel they have contributed to the betterment of humanity when they have given financial aid, which often finds no higher expression than dropping a coin in a panhandler's cup.

There is also the selfish individual who gives only where the compensation is equal or greater in proportion to the contribution. This type of charity sinks to the level of a business deal designed to promote selfish social gains and self-glorification. The person so indulging rarely sacrifices personal time or energy to do a charitable act for another. That person prefers to feel exclusive and aloof from other people. Too busily absorbed in selfish interests, he or she resents being inconvenienced to assist the needy or the handicapped.

Inevitably the time arrives in each of our lives when we face a difficult situation and must call upon someone else for help. Those who have done no charity will then feel humiliated to ask another to render assistance in time of need. Ignorant of the Law of Generosity, such a person attempts to repay favors in terms of material things he or she has gathered and hoarded.

GENEROSITY ⇄ **SELFISHNESS**

Little does that person realize that the deeds of the Spirit are performed without any thought or hope of gain or reward and cannot be compensated for in material terms. True generosity, as with love, is a quality of the soul that expresses kindness, beneficence, mercy, and tolerance.

When we give from the heart we must also receive from the heart. Thus we establish a balance between giving and receiving and maintain the two sides of our consciousness. Only through an awareness of the value of giving does the consciousness receive its greatest power. People who feel they have fulfilled their obligations by making an appreciable contribution to charity should realize that the mere giving of money is not enough. We should give of ourselves and our love, thus causing our consciousness to grow and expand, enabling it to receive the best our fellow humans have to offer.

We are always dealt with generously when our natures become generous, enabling the Divine to have greater expression through our thoughts and actions. Until we reach the plane where there is free giving and receiving, we cannot be assured of lasting security. "He *profits most who serves best*" becomes a living principle and truth when we give not from our hands but from our hearts. It is a law of spiritual compensation that when we give the world our best, the best comes back to us—often in greater abundance.

Therefore, we follow the Golden Rule and do unto others as we would have them do unto us. However, we must use discretion in exercising generosity. Being too generous often debilitates the will of those we desire to help and interferes with the experience necessary for their progress. At the same time an excess of generosity may deplete our own resources that may be destined to promote other worthy causes. Charity is then misdirected and defeats its own purpose, for people become irresponsible, shiftless, and dependent when we absorb all their problems and take on all their burdens.

It requires fine control and discretion never to do for others what they are unwilling to do for themselves. We cannot always compensate for others' ignorance. Furthermore, it is a violation of Law to be kind to one person at the expense of another.

True giving is wisely directed and helps others to help themselves. The person who merely flings a coin to a panhandler is not expressing true charity. On the contrary, the donor often encourages some vice in the individual to whom he or she gives and this endangers society in general.

To those who do not understand the Law of Generosity, this method of giving merely offers balm to their sympathetic nature or their false sense of duty. True charity is not synonymous with mere giving but is distinguished by discerning service, true helpfulness, kindness, and love. We must recognize the great truth that the best and only way to help another is to help oneself, and that poor, neglected individuals need friendliness and understanding more than they need donations.

The mark of true love and service, distinct from the mere pretense for show or personal glory, is that it does not seek praise or publicity. The individual who has the spirit of true service at heart has no desire for commendation and does not boast of good deeds. That person's reward comes from the knowledge of a deed well done. The joy given to others becomes that person's greatest joy. His or her whole nature radiates a spirit of love, kindness, and generosity, thus unintentionally but irresistibly drawing to themselves a rare and divine praise.

Someone who focuses only on personal interests deprives life of its chief charms. Moreover, that defeats the very objectives the person hopes to attain. The natural world has a law that whatever is of no use or serves no purpose will wither and shrivel up. Likewise, a law of our own being holds that if we contribute nothing to the great body of humanity, if we make ourselves of no use or service to others, then those qualities of our nature that promote the development of our higher self will begin degenerating and disintegrating. Thus we lose the chief charm and happiness of life. Then we live only with a small and stunted self. However, when we project our lives into the service of others, in generosity, kindness, and helpfulness, we evolve to a very high plane of existence. Our whole nature will grow and expand, and we will share in the greatest joys of life, our lives becoming rich and beautiful. When we have entered into and taken part in many other lives, as a consequence we share in everyone else's successes, joys, and happiness.

Once we recognize the truth that all are ONE, and that each individual is an integral part of the whole of humanity, then we will strive for the perfection of all people. Just as the imperfect functioning of one bodily organ can impair all function, so in the greater body of humanity when one individual is poor, disheartened or ill, all people in some degree share the suffering. Humanity is created in the image or likeness of God. All of us are the children of God, and therefore all are entitled to share in God's beneficence and abundance. Each individual is but a channel for the outflow of God's abundance to bless all humanity. Just as the individual contributes to the enrichment of others, so all humanity contributes to the individual's well-being.

Once we have purged our minds of hatred, fear, and their allies and have welcomed into our minds love and its companions, we will recognize that these positive attributes of the soul bring a peace of mind and an infinite inspiration that clarify the vision until we can see all the beauties of the earth and recognize humanity's perfection. Each individual is humanity: the ONE in many, the many as ONE. As part of humanity, the individual finds the God-given confidence and ability to go forth and carve out a career of divine usefulness.

In accordance with what we give, and the spirit in which it is given, so shall we receive. If we understand and obey the Law of Generosity-Charity, life is bound to give us what we ask. The Law of Compensation forever operates, and we cannot bargain with life on any other terms. Generosity is a quality of love that gives of itself without any expectation of a material reward— the giving that grants true freedom.

Chapter Twenty
ASPIRATION

Aspiration is the guiding power that directs each of us to strive for loftier things. It motivates an exalted life. It elevates us beyond the plane of selfishness and desire, helping develop a pleasing personality and a noble character.

Desire and aspiration are not synonymous. To desire is to obtain; to aspire is to achieve. Aspiration points to the exaltation resulting from the purification of the soul and not to conditions or endowments that may follow. Whatever we aspire to be we can attain, so far as the spiritual organism is concerned.

Each of us, whether conscious of it or not, is evolving toward perfection. That is the Divine Plan. While there may be many reverses from which we learn valuable lessons and that enable us to advance more rapidly, still it is necessary that each of us retains within our consciousness a picture of the ideal. Jesus exemplifies for Christians the highest human traits of character, and this ideal acts as a guiding light to those who aspire toward perfection.

We should not lose hope if we slip backward or are retarded in our upward climb. Rather we might hold as an ever-guiding light the picture that Christ personified. Thus guided, we may aspire to the heights and ultimately achieve them. An axiom of philosophy states that nothing stands still; either we progress or retrogress. And if viewed in light of history, we may see the great onward movement of consciousness as progressing toward the Divine.

As humanity's intellect has developed, it has been directed

to the accumulation of knowledge and the manipulation of conditions to serve selfish ends. When consciousness evolved in the human plane, life was organized such that survival of the fittest did not predominate. Therefore, the intellect should have changed accordingly. But humanity is slow to learn, and having inordinate greed and desire in their hearts, humans still created evil conditions that became intolerable. As a consequence people revolted.

Revolts always come in natural sequence when evil elements predominate. This is especially true of nations as historically exemplified by the French and Russian Revolutions. When the masses are held in subjection by evil men, they will in time rebel. A perfect example of evil causing an individual to revolt can be found in the biblical story of the Prodigal Son. Intellect had so overshadowed the inherent aspiration within the soul of the Prodigal Son that, finding himself in an intolerable condition, he was compelled to reverse the procedure and turn back toward the Father's house.

Viewed in light of our obedience to or disobedience of the Natural Law, we are all more or less prodigal sons of God. The further we misuse our intellect, the further it leads us away from the Divine and the more desperate our position becomes—until finally aspiration takes us gently by the hand. It then impels us to turn toward the better and more constructive things of life.

Those who live without knowledge of the Laws of the Body, Mind, and Soul may be compared to a ship without a rudder. They are tossed about on the great sea of life by detrimental thoughts and actions that they allow to affect them due to a lack of understanding. A time comes in each of our lives, however, when we aspire to seek the Truth, and in seeking we will find. This brings wisdom, and wisdom soon brings the intellect under control so that it begins to seek the spiritual treasures instead of the material.

Inevitably someone possessing spiritual wisdom always expresses with a conduct many writers refer to as "live and let live." Such souls recognize that God rules the universe under exact law, and they aspire to fully understand and obey the law. In natural sequence comes the knowledge that all are ONE. All are traveling the same path of evolution toward perfection. Knowing that, the soul then begins to enlighten those who are farther back on the path.

There are ignorant, thoughtless, and indolent people who seek the easy way of obtaining what they desire. They speak of luck, fortune, and chance, envying the rich, the talented, the intellectual. They refuse to recognize the trials, failures and struggles that were necessary for others to have accumulated these desirable things. Instead, they feel as if they too should possess these things—but without thought and effort.

Such individuals should realize that the accumulation of either material or spiritual wealth calls for sacrifice, the exercise of faith, and the overcoming of apparently insurmountable difficulties. We cannot gain anything of value and really enjoy it without effort. There are many people on the negative phase of life who endeavor to use their intellect wrongly, and they contribute greatly to the suffering, confusion and chaos of the world.

When we have a sufficiently developed intellect, we know that obeying the laws that govern the body, mind, and soul always brings an immediate reward. Then we automatically choose to align with the positive attributes of life. We begin to eliminate the negative, thereby becoming a powerful factor in the upward progression of humanity.

Each of us who lives by Natural Law will become a center through whom the forces and influences of restoration may operate to conquer evil. Those who have purified their nature may be compared to a dynamo that generates a subtle but powerful force. Guided by wisdom, such a force may set into operation vast mechanisms to produce many forms of good over which no evil shall ultimately prevail. In this way every individual who obeys the Laws of the Body, Mind, and Soul powerfully reinforces the work of restoring such portions of the human race as can be reached.

Our ideals should always conform to the standard of a perfected nature. Each form of life tends toward the state of perfection possible to its kind—or else contravention arrests growth, and degeneration begins. Our individual development is comparable to this. We must either progress to the apex of human excellence or, from any point at which growth is checked, we will retrograde. The individual souls who have purified their natures become cognizant of ONENESS with Divinity and have reached the highest possible point to which aspiration leads.

Spiritual people are the saviors of the world. Just as the material phase of life is sustained and governed by the spiritual, so we, through all our trials, tribulations, and sordid vocations, are nourished by the beautiful visions of great souls who have lived before. For Christians, Christ is the greatest personification of the ideal soul. His conduct in life stands as a beacon to light the path of those followers who are evolving upward. So it is with all the Great Ones.

The composers, sculptors, painters, poets, philosophers, prophets—these are called "the makers of the after-world, the architects of heaven." Our world is more beautiful because they have lived and given us their visions. Without them we would have perished long ago.

Our lives are patterned by our aspirations. We who cherish a beautiful vision in our hearts and live guided by a lofty ideal will ultimately achieve our goals—if we live in obedience to the laws of our being. The highest of those who have walked the earth reveal what we too may some day be. They link us with the Divine and teach us that however pathetically defaced by our infirmities and distorted by our imperfections, we may yet reflect the Image of God.

Chapter Twenty-One
PATIENCE

Patience is the faculty inherent in the human soul that enables us to accomplish our mission without allowing ourselves to be diverted from our purpose by obstacles that could obstruct our path of progression. Patience strengthens our will and fortifies our intellect against life's discouragements. It is a motivating force that enables us to walk steadily forward in our chosen path despite the pitfalls encountered along the way.

Many wander along blind alleys and meet with difficulties that retard advancement. By exercising patience such obstacles can be avoided—or at least they can be overcome—thus maintaining progress. If we lack patience, however, we abandon the project. We are then convinced of our weakness, and advancement is impossible.

The spiritual attitude necessary for those who would advance is one of keen sensibility and endurance. When our soul is peaceful and pure, it awakens to the higher states of consciousness, assuring our entire organism's growth. In the midst of inharmony and chaos, the progressive soul must maintain its calm. Though tested, it must be composed; though deprived, it must be content; though surrounded by sorrow, it must be happy.

A nature that is disinterested in worldly considerations, that vibrates only in response to duty, that is alive and awake to necessities, that is serene and peaceful under any pressure, that is sweet, satisfied and happy in any environment, presents an invulnerable front to evil. The world is full of densest sin,

and life teems with misery. No one can wholly escape its wicked conditions. The only way to wade through its mire without sinking is by responding only when duty calls. Even then, navigating through stormy waters requires patience.

Patience is an indispensable aspect of perseverance. When unforeseen difficulties occur, perseverance helps us surmount them and provides us with the patience and endurance necessary to successfully combat such difficulties. In the face of opposing circumstances, we must guard against the impatience that always arises from forced inactivity. Our frequency and continuity of effort depend on patience, whereas perseverance only gives us the will to make this effort.

Patience enables us to estimate people, conditions, and things in their true light and to guard against the emotional upsets and biased judgment that often cloud the vision. Patience also enables us to choose with discrimination and to carry out with clarity and precision the actions that reason has counseled us to perform.

Our entire world of thought and action should be colored by the quality of patience, yet we readily see that this positive and ennobling attribute is sadly lacking in the home, in the community, and among nations. The need for patience is nowhere more pressing than in the home. Members of a family tend to be hasty and headlong, with little consideration for individual differences. Parents and those entrusted with the guidance and discipline of children are especially guilty of violating the Law of Patience. To be hasty and inconsiderate with children breeds fear, discouragement, self-condemnation. Many an inferiority complex can be attributed to a parent's or teacher's habitual impatient attitude toward a deficiency or a lack in the child. Not only does that parent or teacher violate the Law of Patience but that person also lacks the traits of sympathy, charity, kindness, and duty.

Impatience leads to irritability, which in turn produces anger. Then the mind becomes engrossed in the negative phase of reaction. In the business world there are many individuals who, perplexed and preoccupied with their own problems, exhibit an attitude of impatience toward those they serve. Such an attitude, perhaps bringing temporary satisfaction, will in the end defeat its purpose. Only when we are patient under all circumstances can we maintain harmony.

Even in the realm of healing, where patience should predominate as an indispensable factor in producing results, this constructive force is often lacking. Still ignorant of all the laws involved in healing, many doctors display impatience and irritability toward patients—especially nervous and neurotic cases. In reality the fault lies with the doctor, who has failed to create the composite personality or to instill those concepts necessary to produce constructive results. Some individuals have drifted so far into the negative phase of life that it requires persistent effort and a great deal of patience to bring them back into the positive realm.

When considering the need for patience and its stronger complement endurance, we are apt to think about the greater obstacles and forget the trivial annoyances that beset daily life. Stumbling over petty offenses by allowing them to repeatedly stir our minds into little bubbles of irritation does as much to undermine our nature as the failure to surmount greater errors. When we continuously fail to patiently endure little disturbances, our life forces are scattered and our whole organism is depleted. In this way we become totally unfit to cope with more severe trials, and for such trials we should always be

PATIENCE ⇌ ANGER

prepared. By carefully watching our dispositions and eradicating lesser discrepancies, gradually the force and power will be added with which we can meet and rise superior to any emergency.

Patience rests on faith—in ourselves, in others, and in God. People do not attain to greatness in any line of endeavor without patient, persistent effort. Creative genius has always used patience as an essential factor for achievement. The victory may be at hand, the goal may be in sight, the plan may be nearing its completion, but if we falter or stumble—through impatience—to reach the end, what was within our grasp will end in defeat or disappointment.

Life is one great battle with all its trials and problems. But whatever the necessities of life and whatever the tribulations, small or great, we must remember that unwavering patience and endurance to the end will fortify our character. Our increased strength will move us toward final mastery of all the circumstances that tend to impede our progress.

Every individual can conquer the weaknesses in his or her own nature through a knowledge of and obedience to the laws governing the body, mind, and soul. However, the evils of the world are beyond individual jurisdiction, except where we can serve to help others see the right path. This is best done by example. The world owes its advancement to those souls whose consistent actions personify the positive attributes of faith, hope, charity, patience, and love. When these people are in the majority we may expect the unification of humanity. When people will love one another, they will by their own actions gradually eliminate from the earth all the evil attributes we now know.

As we each become cognizant of our part in the Divine Plan, we cheerfully accept our obligations—and with patience and perseverance perform our allotted tasks. We then realize that the guiding light may often be dimmed by our own restricted vision and that many things which appear painful are in reality designed for our own good—in order to grow and advance. Then we have the faith, hope, patience, and courage to struggle onward, because we know that we are on the path that is built unerringly along the course of the laws of life.

Chapter Twenty-Two
SYMPATHY

Everyone has an instinctive desire to be with other people and to share their feelings. As humanity evolved to a higher state of consciousness, this instinctive trait developed into the attribute of sympathy, based on love, devotion, and human understanding. In its perfected state, sympathy is a necessary prerequisite for promoting the Golden Rule.

Our thoughts and conduct, in many instances, are still controlled by traits from the animal nature, so we are constantly aware of sympathy expressing in its cruder forms. When we confine our feelings, interests, and helpfulness to certain groups or classes, when we allow ourselves to be conscious of kind, then we express a very mediocre and undeveloped form of sympathy. This type of sympathy gives rise to all sorts of racial conflicts and misunderstandings. It causes inharmony and leads to open hostility between races and between groups that hold radically different beliefs, opinions, and social status. This type of sympathy is detrimental to the soul's advancement.

When we no longer discriminate between races, creeds, or color, when our sympathetic consciousness encompasses people in all stations of life, when we radiate a spirit of kindness, charity, patience, and love to the whole body of humanity—then we express sympathy in its highest and most developed stage. Only through awareness of the *oneness* of humanity can we acquire the quality of feeling characterized by mutual understanding and genuine helpfulness toward all people.

Sympathy, in the sense of sorrowing with others, is a viola-

SYMPATHY ⟷ **CRITICISM**

tion of Natural Law and we should not indulge in it. We may exercise it in appreciation of another's suffering, but we should never enlist it to the point of disturbing our own equilibrium. When sympathy disturbs, it weakens, and that which weakens tends to destroy. Through weeping with or for another, we increase our own suffering and make ourselves unfit to help. No circumstance justifies a disturbed attitude.

There comes a time in each person's conscious existence when he or she has risen in consciousness to the extent of feeling a *oneness* with all life. The natural result is to realize that whatever befalls the MANY also harms the ONE. In this type of soul, sympathy reaches its most beautiful expression. The life that exists in the plant, the animal, and the human may then be said to be *en rapport* with this type of evolved soul.

It is only by being aware of separateness and individualized existence that a person feels alone and perhaps afraid. Then all forms of life are separate and distinct entities, some of which that person looks upon with abhorrence. The right kind of sympathy cannot exist in such a personality.

A person who is truly in sympathy with the animal nature cannot ruthlessly blot out its life for mere pleasure. The hunter who delights in the destruction of animal life for sport certainly does not understand that all life is ONE. Being unaware of the laws involved, the hunter merely satisfies an inherited egotistical urge—brought over from the lower states of existence—to match wits against the animal. When we realize that all are ONE, we can no longer ruthlessly destroy life unnecessarily. Rather, we endeavor to make the life of the lower and lesser beings more pleasant. When we reach this point of consciousness, our soul expresses true sympathy. We find a good example of such expression in organizations that fight cruelty to animals, and where individuals devote their time and money to alleviate the suffering of these unfortunate beings.

The needless and unaided suffering of both animals and humans is sufficient evidence to state that sympathy in the true sense is sadly lacking in our vaunted and prosperous civilization. Not only are animals neglected, lacking adequate food and shelter, but the aged and the infirm walk the streets seeking sustenance and the bare comforts of life. Undernourished and underprivileged children fill city slums. Although we have welfare organizations charged with caring for these individuals, some perform their services in a cold, merciless manner and do not alleviate existing conditions. Obviously, the great mass of humanity displays a superficial, sentimental, and insincere sympathetic attitude toward other beings.

As more and more souls advance along the Path of Attainment, spiritual illumination will bring the true kind of sympathy to the earth. Then a great change will be evident. Animals will no longer be ruthlessly slaughtered, the aged and infirm will be freed from their suffering, and no longer will infants be born in filth and squalor. Neither will little children be denied proper nourishment and care. When these reforms are a reality, then true sympathy will have come into its own.

Sympathy often degenerates into a morbid sentimentalism that fails to stimulate healthy effort and encouragement. No true soul will tolerate pity for him or herself, either in their own mind or the mind of a friend—nor will that soul inflict it on another. Average individuals tend to conclude that their problems, struggles, and sorrows are greater than those of their neighbor, and at times greater than any other person's. We must recognize that life is a battle and through our trials, our suffering, our disappointments, and sorrows, we are strengthened and are able to grow spiritually. Each soul has its duties to perform, its lessons to learn, its battles to fight. But through a knowledge and application of the Laws of Life, we gain the faith, hope, sympathetic understanding, courage, and power to meet the challenges that face us throughout life.

The ability to feel for and with others is a vitally important factor in promoting our own advancement and that of humanity. Sympathy for another's problems contributes to unity, harmony, and understanding in a home, a community, or a society. But we must guard against the misuse or abuse of sympathy, especially in the home. Members of a family will discover that they can use sympathy as a tool for enslaving those who love them. It is not uncommon to find a neurotic parent playing upon the sympathy of the children, nor to find a neurotic spouse who enjoys posing as an invalid to gain the mate's sympathetic attitude. Children soon learn that they also can use this illegal weapon to accomplish their selfish objectives. This is a violation of law. While there is a temporary advantage to be gained, the end result is disastrous. When someone places spiritual chains around loved ones by misusing attributes of the soul, that person succeeds only in slowly losing those who love them.

Sympathy, properly used, is an attribute of the soul. Only through our use or misuse of it can it serve as a power for good or evil. Those who realize that all life is ONE will re_og_ nize the evils that exist, and regret that such evils operate to injure many. Immediately those advanced people experience sympathy for the oppressed, and they desire to assist in some way or to contribute something, however little, to alleviate others' misfortunes. All the progress humanity has made toward unity is due to the sympathetic understanding and coopera-

SYMPATHY ⟷ CRITICISM

tive efforts of these advanced souls who have used their time and influence to remedy evil conditions that enslave the masses.

Social progress and individual achievement are not rooted in competition, in the effort to subdue, defeat, or hold down other people. On the contrary, the advancement of each individual and of society rests on cooperation, sympathetic understanding, and reciprocity. By helping others and by being assisted by them in turn, we enlist their capacities, talents, and attributes with our own. As a result we multiply the power of all instead of destroying it by struggling one against the other. No community or nation can stand alone; all are dependent and interdependent.

Only through recognizing the principle of unity can we hope to solve the social problems that face the world. The mass consciousness must become aware of the ONENESS of all humanity, and each individual must recognize that his or her own interests and welfare depend on the welfare of all other members of society.

Sympathy, in its higher sense, is a subtle faculty through which we readily comprehend and appreciate the finer, higher sensibilities of others. It is a faculty through which our own higher sensibilities are in turn comprehended and appreciated. Sympathy invariably accompanies pure love, and lends a sweetness and joy to human relationships unparalleled by any other quality.

Chapter Twenty-Three
NONINTERFERENCE

Each individual soul is destined to fulfill some mission on this earth plane. That soul's life is patterned according to its stage of evolution. The path the soul must travel to fulfill its duties will be burdensome or free from pain and worry to the degree that the individual understands and obeys the laws of its being.

Consider how the rays of the sun individually function to produce part of the great light illuminating the universe. Each ray is an integral unit while being a composite part of the whole—yet they function without interfering with each other. So each individual soul must play its part cheerfully and willingly, contributing to the whole and yet refraining from any interference with another soul's function or mission.

Each person has a role to carry out in accordance with higher laws. To perform that mission, no one should be unduly interfered with. We see so many people who, in their egotistical manner, assume the responsibility of instructing or otherwise impeding the destiny of others who do not desire such instruction. This is a violation of law. God, with Divine Wisdom, has ordained the true course for all, and each of us should be allowed to pursue that course without unwarranted interference.

Had humanity in its original state of innocence not broken this law, it would not have fallen to its present condition. Our calling was to maintain our undisturbed state of mind, to do duty and to grow. But we tried to climb another way and interested ourselves in many things that did not belong to the life of natural progression. Whenever our interests engaged us in pursuits unnecessary to our growth, we disobeyed one of Nature's most essential provisions: noninterference or, in other words, "strictly minding our own business."

It is far more difficult to mind our own business in the turmoil of present conditions than it would have been had humanity not become entangled. Life is now full of disturbing influences, and duties have become complicated and difficult. Yet there is no other constructive course to follow than to perform our duties of promoting self-development without retarding other people's progress or interfering with their well-being.

We should center our hearts and minds on the work assigned to us and should only interfere with the thought or activity of others when such intrusion is warranted. There should be no time to find fault with others, or to pry into their affairs. The world would be an infinitely happier place to live in if only each individual would mind his or her own business. The person who is constantly prying is motivated not by a desire to help someone else, but rather to satisfy curiosity about something that does not concern that person.

The average individual has become so accustomed to interfering, not only with Nature's laws but with innumerable affairs that should not be of concern, that considerable training is usually necessary before he or she realizes the scope of the application of the Law of Noninterference. It is not sufficient for us to refrain from intruding on the affairs of others in deed only. We must abstain in thought, word, and deed. In fact, the first intrusion is always in thought, and much destruction may be wrought even though such transgression does not go beyond the mental plane. Furthermore, it is not only necessary for us to learn not to intrude on others, but we must guard our own territory with equal care. We make the utmost effort to protect earthly possessions, but the treasures of the mind and the soul are often left wide open to intrusion.

When we focus the mind on another person, scanning with interest, speculating on that person's condition or nature, we have penetrated the other's sacred chambers of being. And even though we did not make the greater mistake of criticizing, or especially trying to read or influence that person's mind— both of us are harmed beyond our present power of realization. In whatever way or for whatever purpose we mentally or spiritually intrude on another mind or soul, we unlawfully handle dangerous forces. Whether we do this through mental suggestion or by any other method and whether it's done with or without permission, injury and ultimate destruction surely follow. Both the one who practices these methods and the one practiced upon become victims.

There are always consequences when the mind is carried away from the body and from its activity in abstract thinking or speculation, when it in any way intrudes on another's domain, or when it is influenced or disturbed by being intruded upon or disturbed by its own errors. During these activities, the vibrations thus set in motion pierce, open, and scatter the soul— to the degree that the agitations are violent or prolonged. Thus the soul is constantly exposed to chaotic, contaminating, and deadening conditions that fill the very atmosphere of the earth.

On the streets, in crowds, wherever we go, we are constantly subjected to such interferences. If we wish to preserve and protect our soul, which is our only means for growth, we must avoid promiscuous and unnecessary mingling with people. When called into their midst through duty, we should take the utmost care not to interfere with so much as one thought and we must remain unyielding toward any intrusion from others. When our territory is in any way trespassed on, it is necessary for us to inform the intruder that we will permit no interference. This should be done without any annoyance on our own part and in the wisest way possible to avoid giving offense.

Not only has humanity degenerated to the plane of interfering with neighbors in thought, word, and deed but people habitually intrude on their own being. That interferes with the laws governing the subconscious or automatic phase of mind and body. When we begin tampering with the subconscious functioning of the body, we violate the Law of Noninterference. When our thought process becomes inverted, when we overindulge in self-analysis and introspection, constantly centering our attention on every thought, word, and action, then we become victims of self-condemnation and self-consciousness. All this results from intruding on that phase of our being that should be controlled by the subconscious mind.

Within each of us is a Spiritual Force that directs certain activities: digestion, breathing, rate of the heartbeat, elimination. These functions do not come under the jurisdiction of the conscious mind and therefore should not be interfered with. When the conscious mind constantly interferes, these activities begin to function abnormally—or they cease to function, according to the nature or the degree of interference. The result is various bodily and mental disorders.

When we become acquainted with the Truth about life—the laws governing our being and how to apply them—immediately we want to teach others. But often we find that others are not ready to accept the Truth. Their minds are closed to anything that might militate against their opinions, beliefs, prejudices, and superstitions. They are not eager to seek the lighted path, but rather choose to struggle onward in darkness, adhering to their artificial way of living and thinking. Attempting to sow the seeds of Truth in such infertile mental soil is like "casting pearls before swine." Some people must experience a terrific psychic upheaval resulting from long continued suffering before their minds and souls are awakened and they can understand and obey the Laws of Life.

We should never impose our way of living and thinking on others. Our divine authority over ourselves does not grant us the least jurisdiction over our neighbors. We have the capacity to control our own thinking and to determine what is best for us, but we are not always in a position to judge what is best for our neighbors. When we have evolved to the point of recognizing the unique individuality and divine freedom of every human being, we will then allow others the liberty to think for themselves. The other person may have a better way of life—and may be a step lower or higher on the path—but that is none of our concern.

Helpfulness without interference comes as a natural consequence to understanding the underlying unity of all. We cannot stand aside when others are in distress. Though we cannot always give physical aid, it is our duty to offer our sympathy, kindness, patience, and love.

Forgiveness and love come in the wake of understanding. We must realize that everyone has their own interpretation of life and that the shortest, easiest road for one person is not necessarily the most direct route for another. Each of us has the right and privilege to take our own evolution in hand according to our understanding—so long as we do not interfere with the well-being of our neighbor.

It is not our duty to direct another's life but only to make sure that we are in the right in our relations with others. Before we attempt to force others to pursue our path, we would be wise to investigate their course. Their way might be better for them. The Law of Charity dictates that we must always be ready to help other people to the fullest extent of our ability—but we must never interfere.

Chapter Twenty-Four
KINDNESS

Kindness is a quality of charity and an attribute of love. It is associated with benevolence, consideration, unselfishness, and sympathetic understanding. Its benefits bless not only every phase of human life but they also encompass the far-reaching limits of the animal and vegetable kingdoms. The person who has risen above such destructive traits as greed, selfishness, hatred, jealousy, envy, and has evolved to the plane where generosity, patience, tolerance, sympathy, and love radiate from every thought, word, and deed—such an individual is obeying the laws of their soul and embodies in character and personality the essence of kindness.

Kindness of thought and action should extend to all human beings, especially those who are needy, helpless, infirm, and those who are in any way deprived of a normal, happy existence. Kindness should constitute a predominant trait in the character of all parents, teachers, doctors, and all others entrusted with the care and supervision of children or of any human being. In business, in professional life, in travel, in all social intercourse—at home, in the community, and among nations—consideration and sympathetic understanding of our neighbors is a paramount factor in maintaining peace and happiness in the great human family.

In dealing with our fellow human beings, let us first consider our children. They are but sparks of the Divine Life that have been entrusted to us that we may guide and direct them along the evolutionary highway until they have matured sufficiently to find their own way. Domination and mistreatment of children is cruel despotism designed to promote the selfish interests of individuals who vibrate on a very low plane of existence.

Children's lives are patterned according to Divine Plan, and when we interfere with their evolution by abusing them and using them for our profit and advantage instead of directing them with loving kindness and promoting their welfare, then we violate a divine trust. To our children we must be as a friend with an understanding heart—never a selfish and cruel dictator. No child is a bad child. He or she may have undesirable traits that need to be thwarted or directed into channels of usefulness, but that is our duty—to guide children with perfect kindness and lovingly bring forth an expression of their divine nature.

The aged, the feeble, the poor, and the sick so often become the victims of neglect, indifference, abuse, and even cruelty. Their greatest want is consideration and sympathetic understanding—the little kindnesses that make their burdens a trifle lighter, their lives a bit more cheerful. In each of our lives, somewhere and somehow, we will experience the pangs of weakness and suffering. Then we will long for the touch of a helpful hand, an expression of kindness in our hour of need. Kindness lays the foundation for friendship and constitutes one of its most enduring attributes.

Kindness to others reaps its own reward, for the Law of Compensation provides adequate remuneration for the good that we bestow on others. The benefits we receive from another's thoughtfulness should act as a motivating power for us to treat those whom we contact with consideration and benevolence. When some person has been kind to us, we should express our appreciation by an equal readiness to serve another who needs assistance. Thus the good deeds of the human family are kept in constant circulation, and no individual is left to suffer needlessly. We often receive kindness from people whom we do not have the opportunity to directly return a favor. But we can show our gratitude for these blessings by the good thoughts and deeds that we convey to others. We must remember that we are all ONE, all members of the great body of humanity.

The Law of Kindness extends, also, to the forms of life lower than the human. It is our duty to try and understand the animal, to provide for it when it is deprived of its natural means of self-preservation, and to assist in its evolution. To understand the animal, we must look at its world through its eyes, and in turn we will gain its faith and devotion. We should teach children, in particular, to be gentle with animals and to respect them as part of God's creation. In avoiding harsh or cruel treatment from humans, the animal's mind may possibly be evolved as the animal must learn to think its way out of the abuse. But at the same time that develops the undesirable emotions of fear and hatred in the animal.

In our relations with all forms of life, it is our duty to love and help, to be kind and cooperate in promoting the welfare of all God's creation. All are a part of the One Life. We must not abuse or ruthlessly destroy any living thing—even vegetable life. Through God's Divine Wisdom there is a design and purposeful life for every living organism. We must work in harmony with, not against, the Laws of Nature.

The human soul responds to vibrations, and all vibrations can be classified as being either positive or negative. All destructive emotions are negative in character and invariably produce negative results. Each of us struggles daily to eliminate, or at least control, the destructive attributes that we all possess. Therefore, we should stop and think before allowing ourselves to be impelled by the laws of vibration to vent our baser nature in response to some offending negative thoughts, words, or deeds of others. If we come in contact with people whose conduct could be classified as cruel and abusive, we have two alternatives to consider. One is to recognize the source and ignore it completely. If this is not possible, the second alternative is to follow the axiom: "A soft answer turneth away wrath." But in no event should we allow vibrations of others' evil thoughts or actions to pull us down to their level and act likewise.

Living as we do in a world of constant change and endless variety, we are thrown among souls who are struggling upward. Therefore, we should adapt ourselves to our environment and try to assist those who are lower in the scale.

When we understand the laws of our being, and live in harmony with them, we will find it quite easy to build a wall around ourselves, so to speak, which will keep the negative vibrations of lower souls from dragging us down to their level. The Law of Polarity works in kindness just as it does in every other circumstance and condition concerning life. The path of least resistance is for us to go through life responding to every negative vibration or act, with one equally as crude or as cruel. But that is the coward's way. To recognize the source of evils, and to overcome them by positive thoughts, words, and acts—this is the motive and the essence of kindness.

Let us not just batter our way through life. Instead, let us consider our existence on this earth plane to be a stepping-stone to a higher life, and thereby color our conduct with the noble attributes that characterize the evolving soul.

KINDNESS ⟷ GREED

Often we find individuals who are so deeply submerged in their evil ways that kindness cannot lift them out of their abyss. There is an idea often expounded that love leads the way to a higher life and that love will open the doors to righteousness and purity even in a nature that has closed them by the densest form of evil. This is only one of the fallacies that divert people's minds into wrong channels and keeps them revolving in their unconquered errors. Love is never the forerunner of the Law, but follows in its wake.

Every teacher or reformer should have risen to the plane of love. It is also true that kindness governed by wisdom should be the motive power. Wisdom, however, may demand the greatest severity in the handling of an evil nature. Then, the only kind method is the one that effectually conquers the evil and leaves the individual free. Methods may sometimes be mild and gentle and still be effectual, but there are occasions that demand drastic measures. Whether gentle or loving methods will lead the soul forward or not depends on the extent of its involvement and submissiveness, and on its obedience to guidance.

When right and justice are submerged, kindness will be of no advantage. Love may stand and beat in vain at the door of a nature that is governed by selfishness. Under such conditions the sword must be used. And love is not the sword but the motivating power behind it—and the balm that heals the wound. Whatever resists the law of right will smother love, and those who try to use love's methods indiscriminately in evil conditions will find themselves like a child beating flames with a toy.

Kindness, operating under the light of love and guided by wisdom, may take many forms. When we act according to individual whim, independent of either love or wisdom, we do not express kindness but a mere imitation which often does more harm than good. Only when we are obedient to the laws of our being can we always know how to be truly kind. To gratify an indulgent nature is not kindness. That which helps the soul to rise above desire, or rid itself of weakness, is truly kind.

To be kind, we must first be just and demand justice, to do right and demand right in return. We are kind when we can be merciful, charitable, and generous, whenever the occasion permits without cost to the higher nature. We are kind when we bless where such blessings enrich the soul and lead it toward the light. Let each of us who would grow be kind in nature, consciousness, speech, and acts—as opportunity permits, as love prompts, and as wisdom guides.

KINDNESS ⟵⟶ GREED

Chapter Twenty-Five
COURAGE

Courage is the attribute of the soul that gives us the strength, power, and endurance to overcome or surmount obstacles, weakness, hardships, failure, loss, disappointment, crisis—any force, circumstance, condition, person, or thing that tends to impede our progress or interfere with our well-being.

Many types of courage find expression on every plane of our being—physical, mental, and spiritual. Courage is closely associated with bravery, gallantry, valor, and heroism. Bravery implies fearlessness in the face of danger, whereas courage may be shown in spite of fear. Gallantry is "dashing courage." Valor defies danger, and heroism signifies self-denial and self-sacrifice in the face of danger. Heroism is a spontaneous act of extraordinary courage.

There is always a motivating force behind courage that determines its nature and intensity. Aside from the instinctive traits that motivate someone's courageous action, all human beings are endowed, according to their stage of evolution, with attributes of the soul such as love, faith, devotion, loyalty, and unselfishness. Those qualities stimulate the noblest form of courage. Spiritual courage is founded on faith and unselfishness. It accompanies loyalty, devotion, and personal commitment. Those causes, persons, and values that are nearest and dearest to our hearts inspire the strongest and most enduring courage.

Courage is a vibratory emotion of a positive nature, and all souls within its sphere of radiation are instantly attracted to it.

COURAGE ⟺ HYPROCISY

When we face a dangerous or difficult situation courageously, we transmit the same feeling to others. Thus when we consistently exercise this positive attribute when meeting life's problems and adversities, we benefit—and so do all those in contact with us. Courageous men and women never indulge in self-pity or complacency. Their souls shine as ever-guiding lights to lead others out of darkness and confusion. Life has many trials and tribulations, and it is only the courage to face these and master them that allows us to strive upward.

When courage is lost, all is lost. We become weaklings, afraid to meet the test of life. We see examples of this every day in those people who have lost their courage, who have given up hope, who allow themselves to sink to the depths of human society. The person who indulges in self-pity is naturally a coward. When our power and energy become inverted, when we become overly concerned about ourselves, then we have incapacitated ourselves for brave and daring action. Then our inevitable reaction to danger and difficulty is not courage but alibis and escapes.

Courage is a great constructive power in overcoming the negative and destructive forces within the self. It is an essential factor in self-control and self-discipline. As long as people succumb to the desires, urges, and tendencies of their animalistic nature, they will continue to vibrate on a low plane. Only as we learn, through courageous thought and action, to control and redirect these tendencies, will we evolve to a higher plane of existence. Humanity's duty is not to live for itself alone. Recognizing the ONENESS of all life, we must exercise courage in controlling those habits and traits that tend to degrade our nature. As a consequence, we will aspire to live according to our highest ideal of our relation to God and to other people.

COURAGE ⇌ HYPROCISY

In the make-up of each person's character, we find the *carnal person* and the *spiritual person* constantly struggling for supremacy. The carnal person embodies all the destructive, worldly traits that tend to lower human nature. The spiritual person represents all the attributes of the soul, which shine like a light to direct the soul on the upward path. Self-control and self-discipline do not mean self-repression but, to the contrary, spell power for self-expression gained through exercising courage in overwhelming the destructive forces within ourselves and within other people.

It requires courage to shoulder our responsibilities, to work out our own problems. It is so much easier to burden another person, often taking advantage of their friendship and love. As the saying goes, misery loves company. Selfish, cowardly people don't possess the character to fight their own battles—physical, mental, or spiritual. When inconvenienced, when in distress, they never fail to share their discomfort with those about them, disrupting their peace and happiness.

So many individuals delight in posing as martyrs, but such behavior clearly indicates a weakness of character and a lack of courage. To assume the role of suffering innocence is a violation of the Law of Courage, and anyone who pities him or herself is lost. What more destructive habit for mind and soul could we indulge in than to nurse our nerves, coddle our whims, or baby our sins?

We are entitled to peace and happiness, and it takes courage to face the evils of the world and rise above them. When people and things around us become irritating and depressing, we must adapt ourselves and rise superior to those annoying elements in our environment or in other personalities. To become weak and indulge in the destructive forces of the mind can only result in our own downfall. People of courage defend their rights, control their emotions, and ever maintain a happy state of mind.

To be pleasant when everything is "rosy" is simple, but to be good-humored when things are getting rough requires that we exercise courage. In meeting the challenges of our environment, we must either conquer them or they will conquer us. Either we must be the victor over circumstance or else become its victims. Most people follow the path of least resistance. They long for a life of ease, free from struggle and pain, and were it within their power to plan and arrange the conditions and circumstances of their lives, nothing would interfere with their ease and comfort. Consequently, the most stimulating elements for growth and development of body, mind, and soul would be eliminated.

God's Divine Wisdom has designed and planned a world in which struggle and effort are compensated for by character development. The great discoveries, inventions, and productions in every field of human endeavor have been possible through the heroic efforts of those brave souls who have recognized that growth and achievement lie in meeting and mastering the conflicting forces and difficulties of Nature and humanity.

The height of humanity's possibilities and the fullness of its power rest on our awareness of the world of realities in which we might grow and develop. They also rest on our capacity to meet and master the challenges of life. Many people become dwarfed in mind and darkened in spirit because they live in a world of unrealities. They lack the courage to seek enlightenment and to struggle through the mire of opposing forces in conquering their environment. They lack the faith in themselves, in other people, and in God to strive in cooperative effort until the final victory is achieved. People who can see the challenging vision of the far horizon, prepare themselves and press on—growing in wisdom and experience each day as they stretch toward the mount of conquest—will ultimately reach their goals.

In our daily lives we meet obstacles that seem so great we wonder what's the use of going on. We are inclined to give up, to blame our bad luck, and to look pessimistically on the world. On such occasions we should recognize the fact that life was, is, and always will be full of obstacles. We should use these experiences to gain more and more courage so that, as we evolve, we will have an abundance stored up.

When we recognize that this universe is governed by God's Immutable Laws and that nothing happens by chance, that each difficulty met with has its own purpose in the Great Plan—then we cease to rebel against the great scheme of things. Through our struggles in this world of unharnessed Nature and endless difficulties, we gain experience and wisdom. Thus we evolve to higher and higher planes of existence until we attain our destiny as Children of God.

As we grow spiritually, we acquire a better understanding of other people. And when we take the material of this world and through it allow our souls to find expression, then we have contributed something of value to humanity. Mental and material wealth contribute to character development only to the degree that they are used as a medium in serving the Divine for the good of humanity, and as a tool to promote our personal evolutionary progress. All of our resources are temptations to selfish desire, and unless we use them constructively they will lead us on the downward path. We must constantly exercise courage to guard against the downward pull of mental or material riches.

There is an apt saying: *The soul would have no rainbow had the eyes no tears.* Many individuals owe their successes and their triumphs to tremendous difficulties, and some of our greatest contributions to life have been the outcome of the pressure of suffering. Many people who are physically handicapped display unusual courage. Their other powers seem to become magnified, their limitations motivating a courage that strengthens their mental and spiritual capacity for self-expression. Some of the greatest masterpieces have been the expression of individuals who have been deprived of some physical possibility—individuals who defied Fate and had the courage to overcome their handicaps.

When pain, suffering, misfortune or calamity threaten our peace and happiness, and at times our very existence, then let us have the courage to fight onward. By overcoming the demons of fear and worry that rise on such occasions, they cannot subdue our minds and dim the visions of our souls. Much of our misery and depression in this life is due to our own violation of the laws of our being. As long as we allow people and things to influence us to a spirit of fear, then chaos, confusion, and destruction will be rampant in the world. But when we radiate a spirit of faith, love, and courage, when we embody in our souls all the noble attributes that lift humanity above the plane of selfishness and desire, when we keep our faces turned toward the sunshine—then the shadows will fall behind us.

Through the Law of Opposites and the Law of Relativity, we obtain our sense of beauty and goodness. And through the operation of these laws we are provided with an ever-present stimulus for courageous thought and action. Some people get little joy out of life because they have few appreciations. Their interests are confined to a small selfish circle. Outside of that limited sphere, their eyes are blind and their ears are deaf to the appeals, attractions, and challenges in every field of human enterprise. They do not possess the courage to pioneer new ideas or movements, to explore strange regions, to invent different ways and means, or to alter the accepted order of things to any degree.

We have countless examples of brave souls who have exposed themselves to criticism, condemnation, and abuse of the most diverse kinds, while timid souls, who actually admire the others' courage, hold back their approval in order that they themselves might stand safely back among the masses. The universe is a vast panorama of contrasts and variety filled with endless appeals and challenges for heroic effort, but our minds must be open and our souls must be generous, imbued with faith, love, and courage, so that we might combat the obstacles of life and ultimately achieve our goals.

Chapter Twenty-Six
FORGIVENESS

The latent attribute of forgiveness was brought to the threshold of consciousness when humanity first transgressed the Laws of being. The friction, pain, and penalty resulting from the violation brought physical and mental suffering. In its distress, humanity repented the wrong action and recognized the need to be forgiven. Only someone who has reached a state of perfection is free from the ignorance, temptation, and corruption that leads to transgression of law. However far along the path toward perfection we may have traveled, unless we have reached the summit, we still make mistakes. We have our shortcomings and weaknesses, and will always need to be forgiven for the faults, flaws, and offenses that characterize our thoughts and actions. Thus anyone who cannot forgive others breaks the bridge over which they, too, must inevitably pass.

Kindness, sympathetic understanding, charity, love—these are the attributes that prepare the way for forgiveness. As long as we have need to be forgiven, we must pardon others for their trespasses. It takes an open mind and a kind and generous heart to view the situation through another's eyes, to get another's outlook, perspective, viewpoint. It is so easy to condemn someone else for their iniquities. Let us first analyze the circumstances that led to the wrongdoing, because we are all only human. The cruel despots of hatred and revenge are ever ready to sway the mind in its judgment and to blind the soul from seeing the good there is in people. Let us not stoop to these destructive forces when evil torments us.

FORGIVENESS ⬄ PREJUDICE

Sometimes people hurt us intentionally and grievously, and often without any expression of regret. Whether we should overlook and forgive such offenses depends on the circumstances and the motive behind the thought or action. We should not be vindictive, for revenge is a boomerang that harms the person who indulges in this destructive force more than it does its intended victim. People who are not content until they get even with their aggressors hold themselves on a low plane, bringing illness to body, confusion to mind, and darkness to soul. Whether to repay injuries by justice or kindness depends on the nature and extent of the law's violation.

We need to differentiate between two types of vindication. The method of revenge expressed in the maxim "an eye for an eye and a tooth for a tooth," prevailed when the human race lived in ignorance of its relationship to one another. But as humanity became more intelligent, it gradually developed another method. Jesus taught this by saying, "If a man shall strike you on one cheek, turn the other." One method expresses love, the other hatred. Therefore, we must choose which method to employ in our relationships.

Those who harm us by word or deed, and who do so knowingly, are violating Natural Law to their own detriment. When we are aware of this, then instead of harboring a grudge against them or desiring revenge, we should realize that the very laws they violate will bring inevitable retribution. Therefore, we need not intensify their punishment. Rather we should realize that the one who injures or damages does so in ignorance. Such action should incite our pity. Maintaining this attitude, it is easy for us to do as Jesus did when nailed to the cross. Looking down in his agony on those who had tortured him, he realized that they were as little children, unaware of the enormity of their crime. Thus he exclaimed: "Forgive them, Father, for they know not what they do."

This does not mean that we should look at all harm in this manner. There are some people whose souls are so perverted that they intentionally and deliberately bring injury to others to advance some evil purposes of their own. Such individuals should be brought to justice for the deliberate, premeditated evil they cause.

We cannot hold someone accountable for unavoidable ignorance since we are all human, and to some extent subject to violation of law. However, it is our duty to become as informed as possible regarding the truth about life—to seek knowledge of the laws of our being and obey them as much as possible.

With wisdom comes understanding, and when we understand the laws we cannot willfully violate them without expecting due punishment. Surely we cannot hope to transgress Nature's laws without the inevitable penalty or suffering. The Law of Compensation makes no exceptions. Despite good intentions, we may bring injury and even tragedy into others' lives. In a complex society, ignorance and carelessness may do as much damage as willful aggression, especially where powerful individualists exert their influence over many people. To be able to choose between right and wrong action, we must know what is right under the circumstances and act accordingly. When ignorance causes violation of law, we can be more generous in imposing a penalty or in granting forgiveness. Those possessing knowledge and authority have a duty to instruct and aid others who live in ignorance and darkness. It is contrary to the Divine Plan to condemn and refuse to assist those who are ready to learn.

Everyone possesses certain ideals and aspirations. To the

degree that we become conscious of these ideals and aspirations, they create a sense of obligation within our consciousness. The more sensitive a person's nature, the more acutely he or she will feel the defeat or inner discord when choosing unwisely or violating the laws of being—and the greater will be the desire for forgiveness. When we evolve to the point where we can choose with wisdom and discriminate between right action and wrong action, we will have learned to take full responsibility for our actions and for the effects those actions may have on others. Then we will have broadened our vision, deepened our understanding of human nature, and increased our power of forgiveness. But even the wise person must guard against the sense of guilt or remorse that becomes inverted and results in self-condemnation.

To forgive a wrongdoing, sin, or mistake implies we are liberated from every sense of condemnation, that we are free from a sense of punishment, fear and morbidity. We cannot be forgiven as long as we retain within ourselves the burden of condemnation. To gain freedom from the relentless pressure of condemnation, we must learn to forgive ourselves and to forgive others.

Self-condemnation can bring more pain and suffering than any outside destructive force. Continually indulged in, it stunts the growth of the whole organism—body, mind, and soul. If we sincerely regret some wrong thought, word, or deed, the logical action is to analyze the situation and profit from the failure or transgression. That means we strengthen our powers in a firm resolve to avoid making the same mistake again. Jesus understood that a sense of guilt was at the root of most illnesses, and he often told those who came for healing: "Your sins are forgiven you."

FORGIVENESS ⟷ PREJUDICE

The Christian Bible further urges: "Let not the sun go down upon your wrath." In other words, let us make peace today with others in our lives, for tomorrow may be too late. During our brief stay here on this earth, why should we indulge in hating anyone? Let us instead exchange a good deed for an evil one, forgiving the other person for their offense, and in so doing, contact that person's soul and lead them toward the light. If we continuously emphasize the good in a person, the positive forces will soon predominate. They will then assume command of the soul, liberating it from the fetters of the evil forces that previously held it in bondage, ignorance, and darkness.

Sometimes forgiveness may be difficult or even appear inadvisable, but it is the charitable thing to do. Anyone who never forgives should make sure that no occasion arises when he or she will require forgiveness. People who relieve their conscious thought of all injuries and who refuse to indulge in revenge or animosity have elevated themselves to an exalted place. There, evil forces can no longer disturb their peace or interfere with their happiness.

So long as evil natures endure, so long as we are caught, bound, and subjected to habits and passions that enthrall us and rob us of our self-possession, forgiveness must repeat itself. Whenever the nature is penitent, we must give it another opportunity. Unforgivingness can never be approved, whether the wrongdoer is penitent or not. Unforgivingness is born of a deep sense of injury, which is usually brooded over and always excused in the mind of the one thus indulging. It is a type of solace for self-pity and has no place in the progressive life.

Anyone who has risen above others' petty offenses never allows another's wrongdoing to influence his or her nature to the least degree. We can have nothing to do with any evil directed toward us, other than to protect ourselves to the best of our ability, however the occasion demands, and to preserve our attitude from being disturbed.

We must learn to forgive and forget others' offenses and realize that true forgiveness flows only from a strength and greatness of soul. The person with true forgiveness is conscious of their own force and security, and therefore above the temptation to resent any attempt to interrupt their happiness.

Chapter Twenty-Seven
DUTY

When reason is given to a latent soul, the individual is endowed with the power of free choice in order to learn through experience. To the degree that we view humans as free creative personalities, we must interpret duty in light of how it relates to individual will and impulse. From this vital relationship, duty derives its moral quality.

Our duties depend on our spiritual standing, the conditions to which we have become subjected, our personal ideals, and the social standards that influence our thinking and activity. Duty is largely an individual matter, for what one person regards as a moral obligation, another person may not. An act becomes our moral duty according to our standard of right and wrong and in keeping with our personal ideals.

There is much misunderstanding about the topic of duty. We may do many things from a misconceived sense of duty while simultaneously neglecting actual responsibilities. Individuals who always strive for perfectionism are burdened with superficial and imaginary duties and are constantly submerged in a turmoil of nervous activity, hoping to fulfill all their obligations in the line of duty. Many people, also, accept their conscience as a guide to conduct, and are disastrously conscientious. Enslaved by a misdirected sense of duty, they become the victims of worry and remorse over unimportant issues and insignificant details.

Although the nature of duty is decidedly individual, still we each must live so as to receive sufficient wisdom for guidance.

There is, however, a general rule for all. That rule asserts it is everyone's duty to cease all mental and spiritual action that interferes with growth of character. Furthermore, we must make our physical conditions or surroundings conform to the best interests of progression, to the extent possible.

There is provision for the physical plane because many people are so encumbered by conditions and relationships that it is impossible for them to free themselves immediately. Whatever our environment, however, we should do the utmost to govern our mind and purify our soul.

To reach the highest standard, we should closely analyze ourselves to see that we are not held in detrimental conditions through selfishness or desire. Often it is necessary to choose between two evils. In this case, we should choose in favor of the thing that is less indulgent to a selfish nature—whether that nature is our own or someone else's.

Sometimes the guise of duty holds us in bondage to others, and thereby prevents our progression. Such false duties should not hold us, and sometimes we must use severe methods to free ourselves. The mere fact of relationship should not prevent us from arranging our affairs to best conform to our development. We should measure duty by something more profound than earthly ties. One person has no right to be an obstruction in another's path through the sense of ownership accompanying such relationships. Those who are trying to purge their lives of all that is false and detrimental should disregard the selfish and detrimental demands made by a father, mother, son, daughter, sister, or brother who refuses to live the true life. The people who are truly related to us are those with whom we are united in progression.

Humanity's duties extend to the physical, mental, and spiritual planes. It is our duty to utilize our powers to best assist others, to develop our own higher self, and to meet the challenges of life. In short, it is our duty to seek knowledge and understanding of the laws governing our own being—body, mind, and soul—and to obey them, thus becoming an outlet or channel for Divine expression.

Ignorance and transgression of the Laws of Life bring confusion, pain, and suffering. But a knowledge of and obedience to the laws shows wisdom and results in the highest possible development attainable on this earth plane. When an individual lives in antagonism to the rest of the universe, his or her growth is checked. We must maintain harmony among all the parts of the whole, and we each must contribute our dutiful share.

Each of us has the latent capacity to know and utilize the Laws of Life, but this power must be consciously developed. People whose consciousness has become fully aware of the Divine within itself, and who project this realization into their lives, have the greatest power.

Each of us has an assigned job to do in this world—a mission in life, a duty we must perform to the best of our ability. We may be inclined to believe that one type of work is more commendable than another in the eyes of the Divine. But whether our work is humble or dignified, perfect or imperfect, Divine or secular, depends on the manner in which we perform it. Great souls have labored at menial jobs faithfully and well, realizing that these tasks were just stepping-stones, necessary experiences in their evolution. The merit or fault, success or failure of a work is determined by the spiritual qualities accompanying it. "*It matters not to God or the world whether a man is a butcher or a bishop, but it matters whether he is a good butcher or a good bishop.*"

A Power higher than we are plans our duties and destinies. Each person has a calling, a talent, a mission designed to assist that individual in his or her progress. These may not be of our own choice nor according to our likes or dislikes. But our task may be merely a preparation for greater work. Therefore, we must not object when we are assigned a job that is difficult, unpleasant, or contrary to our wishes. When we are ready for a better type of work, it will be placed before us.

The honest and faithful performance of duty is rewarded by the knowledge of a job well done. Resentment often tempts us in the throes of suffering or punishment, but out of our misery some good may come. Severe punishment often awakens those who refuse to see the light. We are just souls animating these bodies—instruments of the Divine. When we fail to perform our duties, when we become impatient, negligent, and faultfinding, then we are straying from the path that leads to a higher life.

Not only are we obligated to pursue the course of action that is in harmony with right reason, but we must also exercise caution not to overdo duty. Under existing circumstances of human life, the latter is perhaps the more difficult phase of the Law of Duty to thoroughly understand and properly apply. So unconscious has humanity become of the source of its helpfulness, and so closed are the avenues through which such aid may come, that many people are almost defeated by their environment. The pressure is so great that enforced duty carries them far beyond the natural limit.

We should never be called upon to sacrifice physical, mental, or spiritual welfare in performing duties. The fact that this is necessary is only the web in which the human race has entangled itself. Here, as always, we must face the condition as it is, and to the best of our ability observe the laws that create freedom.

In regard to helping others, we must learn to estimate accurately any modifying circumstances so we may determine when duty calls and how far it extends. There is always a price to pay for everything we do in this world: The Law of Compensation forever operates. Every act of life costs life forces, and our capacity to receive is necessarily limited. Regardless of Nature's abundant supply, our expenditure must never exceed our accumulation. If, at any time, we use or scatter our life forces more rapidly than we gather or appropriate them, we become impoverished. We must consider what we can afford. It is a well-known fact that cost is always estimated in terms of expended material wealth, but it is necessary to make much closer divisions when soul or life elements are in question.

It is humanity's duty to develop its own potentialities—physical, mental, spiritual. As we become aware of the ONENESS of all life, we recognize our duty to all God's creation. We then begin to control and eliminate the negative forces that bring discord, suffering, and unhappiness into our own life and the lives of others. The spark of Divine love begins to flame forth in our soul, growing in intensity and magnitude until it embraces all life. It is our duty to be happy and to provide an atmosphere of peace, joy, and devotion toward others.

When love, unselfishness, and all the other attributes of the soul permeate the atmosphere in which we must work, then the crudest and humblest task becomes exalted. In performing our duties, we experience a supreme satisfaction knowing that we are promoting not only our own advancement but that of others in accordance with the Divine plan.

Chapter Twenty-Eight
LOVE

True love is of the Divine and is the highest attribute of the human soul. Among people, it is the harmonious vibrations between bodies, minds, and souls. Love is the dynamic principle of life itself. It is the interior element of the creative principle and the central fire of the soul. Had human nature remained true enough to itself to have permitted the development and free activity of this mighty force, all humanity would have been vitalized and glorified by its influence, and nowhere would it have been lacking. The Golden Rule would be a natural function of human life, and peace, happiness, and good-will would breathe in every soul.

Love is the most powerful spiritual force in the world. It embraces within its sphere of radiation all the other positive soul qualities: faith, hope, charity, kindness, patience, sympathy, forgiveness, unselfishness, courage. Love is the expression of the Divine through the medium of the human soul. It constitutes the most vital energy required for our spiritual advancement. The farther we advance in the scale of evolution, the more spontaneous and far-reaching will be our expression of love.

Among people with limited understanding, a sort of chemical affinity between bodies draws one to another. This is misconstrued as love. Individuals may be attracted toward each other through the physical alone, through the mental alone, or only through the spiritual. Various combinations of the three may also be formed through which people are attracted. When union takes place through only the senses or physical organism,

LOVE ⟺ HATRED

the vilest passions of perverted nature counterfeit love and are soon expended in satiated desire. From this state, under the pressure of the accompanying passions of anger, jealousy, and hatred, it is an easy step to tragedy and crime.

Unions formed through mental attractions, or attraction of minds of like character, are less destructive. But such contact does not awaken love. It gives rise to an attachment born only of the gratification of blended intellectual tastes and qualifications. No union can be blessed with pure love that is influenced by either sensual or intellectual gratification. Indulgence of desires on any plane contradicts natural law and is detrimental. Those who are attracted through their spiritual natures do not necessarily love. They may be kindred souls on a low plane, but love cannot live in other than a pure atmosphere. Whether the emotion felt by like souls is pure love or not depends on their standards. Individuals may unite through a harmonious blending of physical, mental, and spiritual natures, and even then know nothing higher than a set of emotions generated by the contact of like elements.

In these examples we readily see how the law of attraction, operating under various superficial influences and associations, may draw together all kinds of people. Many combinations are thus formed which by their very nature must be inharmonious, inconsistent, and temporary.

The emotions between the sexes are usually nothing more exalted than chemical affinity or magnetism on another plane. In addition, the attachments between parents and their children—and among all sorts of earthly relationships where love is said to exist—are mostly formed of far baser metal than the gold of pure love. Almost all parental love, which is considered the highest type of earthly love, is selfish and binding to the child. Filial love is equally selfish and exacting. When criticism, condemnation, selfishness, and general inharmony characterize family life, the attachments are little more than fleshly ties.

If desire, jealousy, or any form of selfishness surrounds or colors the feeling called love, know that they mark an attachment of a much lower order. If we grieve for the loss of a loved one, for example, our love is selfish. When there is a bond between two people, and a necessary separation ensues, grief on the part of either one darkens or binds both. When death comes, sorrowing relatives and friends hold the soul earth-bound and in the condition of suffering and darkness that belong to this plane.

Love is absolutely unselfish and never binds its object. If our love is pure, we release the selfish ties that bind and give our loved one, whether on the earth or having passed beyond, freedom to advance as Nature guides, or to go and come in response to duty or the pursuit of their higher well-being.

Of all the attributes preserved in human nature, the quality of love is the most misrepresented and least understood. When we learn that love can become active only in a soul that is pure, and that it does not cooperate with the errors of an artificial nature, then we may understand to what extent it has been counterfeited.

As desire and selfishness colored the nature, and their long train of evils crowded in, they smothered flames of love. Only a spark has remained to cast its faint glow through the darkness. But despite all the evils that have surrounded and stifled human love, its fires have never been wholly quenched in the human soul. The reason dissatisfied natures delude themselves by grasping counterfeit emotions is to fill the void felt by that soul whose love nature is not dead but submerged. The fact that love has never been quite lost to the soul has preserved humanity from utter desolation. By its remaining warmth hope has lived—hope that leads to light and faith.

True love emanates from the Divine. It is the act of self-giving through creation, the impartation of the Divine through the human. Love is a complete unity with life, and only as the soul becomes conscious of its ONENESS with all that lives, can it express genuine love. When we realize that God and humanity are One, then we shall love humanity as an expression of God, and God as the Life Principle in all creation.

The nature of true love is to give and to bless, as the sun gives its light and the flowers their fragrance. It does not demand or require anything in return. False love centers on itself. It is selfish, binding, and exacting. Since it is not genuine, it is narrow, shallow, temporary. To the degree that it is influenced by the attending evils of criticism, condemnation, and jealousy, it will ultimately turn to hatred. False love gives only with the thought of getting something in return. It lives for itself and its own gratifications.

We indulge in counterfeit love when our love is confined only to certain individuals or groups; when it is colored by our tastes, opinions, and prejudices; when it is restricted by custom, belief, social status, nationality. People have always thought of love as something we can express or repress at will. Thus we classify and segregate people according to our likes and dislikes. We show kindness and consideration to our intimates, but to strangers we are cold and indifferent. We are taught to love our country, our religion, our way of thinking and living, while those who differ from us in nationality, in religious training, in custom and point of view become the victims of our disdain and bitter aversion.

LOVE ⇌ HATRED

Two opposing forces cannot flow from the soul at the same time. Love is the opposite of hatred, and it is contrary to the Law of Opposites for the vital energy of life to be malevolent and yet also be benevolent. Therefore, Jesus said, "Love your enemies; love those that hate you." The emotion of love is an electromanifestation from the brain that is stronger than that of hatred. Hence, it overcomes the hate. When a soul is animated with love, it radiates the warmth of its feeling, and it blesses and inspires whomever it contacts. And the object of its beneficence will reflect back the same ennobling influence.

True love expresses itself in the growth and development of personality. Through Divine love we become conscious of tremendous power, amazing capacities, higher aspirations, and greater freedom. As we begin to love all life as an expression of the Divine, we find it easier to perform our daily tasks and to meet life's challenges. Other individuals who appear lower in the scale no longer obstruct our advancement. Through love we rise above the baser elements in ourselves and in others. We become conscious of greater beauty and joy in the universe, qualities that were shrouded from our view as long as we lived in the darkness of evil tendencies.

Counterfeit love stunts our growth on every plane of being. It warps our personality and darkens our soul. Love must be the master of the self. It must control the passions of the body, the thoughts, the imagination, and the longings of the soul. It never expresses itself on a low plane, but leads us away from our baser selves to the realms of loftier expression.

This beneficent force brings health to the body, peace to the mind, and strength and freedom to the soul. Wherever the atmosphere around human beings is permeated with a spirit of love, there strife and struggle will end, enmity will be lessened, evil will be overcome. There, people will arrive at an understanding of each other that can result only in lasting peace, cooperation, and happiness.

As long as negative forces of the mind, such as greed, jealousy, selfishness, prejudice, etc., dominate and control human minds, discord, suffering and unhappiness will reign in the home, the community and among nations. Only as each of us recognizes and applies the laws of life—lending all our efforts toward battering down negative attributes that tend to hold us on a low plane and ultimately destroy us, releasing the hidden power of love and allowing it to find expression in the well-being of other people and in the advancement of our own soul— only then can humanity hope to be happy and free.

One of the most beautiful qualities of love is the faith it creates—in God, in humanity, in the purpose and possibilities of life. As the Christian Bible says, *"Perfect love casteth out fear."* And with fear's opposite, faith, comes courage and strength. Courage is the essence of sacrificial love, and without it we could never elevate ourselves to higher planes of living and thinking. When we truly love a person, a priceless possession, a truth, we are willing and ready to fight for it. There is always some truth, dimly perceptible, gleaming forth to light our pathway when we love it to the extent of dedicating our lives to it. Every truth that has been responsible for higher achievement has risen from individual sacrifice. It has been said that truth has many names, but it is best known as *Love.*

Genuine love has a powerful attraction that brings together those who are Divinely inspired to create something worthy of love. The bonds of loyalty among souls who are thus united cannot be broken. If our creative capacity is endowed with love, it will release untold benefits to bless humanity. However, if those who possess great powers choose to exercise them in

LOVE ⇌ HATRED

conformity with the grosser attributes of humanity—such as greed, selfishness, lust—then discord, suffering, and destruction will be the inevitable consequence.

How cold and barren and meaningless is life where love is wanting? What satisfaction or reward comes in performing tasks or rendering service for mere material gain, or in the line of duty, without inspiration of love? When human souls mingle among each other, or in groups, societies, organizations or nations, their actions are governed by either greed or love. If love does not predominate, then someone suffers to the degree that another gains.

As the soul conquers its weaknesses, meets the requirements for progression and returns to its pure nature, love, fanned by the breath of purity, awakens and flames into being. The life that is lived in accordance with the Laws of the Body, Mind, and Soul, and which embodies all the other positive attributes, culminates in love.

Love is the fruition of the purified nature. When individuals who have so risen come together and their pure elements connect through the law of spiritual affinity, love becomes active. Then, true to its nature, it radiates and blesses whomever it touches.

Pure love responds only to the union of souls who are characterized by the highest attributes. Their capabilities of pure love are measured by the degree to which the lower elements have been misplaced by the nobler qualifications. Inharmony results from a conflict of elements governed by selfish, crude and uncontrolled natures. When individuals unite through the blending of souls that are unselfish, self-possessed, and pure, the mental and physical organisms are subjugated and harmonized.

If we desire love, we must set up a "polarity" to attract love.

LOVE ⇌ HATRED

This powerful force can awaken the greatest that is in our souls, and thus it is the medium for remarkable spiritual development. The law of spiritual affinity cannot have its perfect way until we have lifted our natures from the plane of selfishness and desire, and our spiritual natures have become pure enough and vital enough to govern our whole organism and overcome attraction on any other plane.

When individuals unite under the perfect working of this law, love seals the union with a bond that endures not only during earth life but through eternity.

CONCLUSION

NATURAL LAWS
AND THEIR RELATION
TO HEALTH AND DISEASE

In considering the subject of Natural Law, it is well to review what is meant by *law*. One eminent writer defined it as "an ascertained working sequence or constant order among the phenomena of Nature." Webster describes it as "any force, tendency, propensity or instinct, natural or acquired." Such definitions, although technically correct, convey a cold, mechanical meaning that almost seems tinged with fatalism. Instead, consider this explanation: *Law is the uniform and orderly method of the omnipotent God. Natural Law that pervades the physical, mental, and spiritual kingdoms is God in manifestation.*

Only a few centuries ago the prevailing opinion held that such events as the movement of the earth and other planets through space, the ebb and flow of the tides, the growth of plants and trees, and the obvious multiform operations of gravitation and cohesion were phenomenal. Scientists regarded everything immaterial as being beyond the pale of law. Theologians viewed the spiritual domain as above law, or supernatural. The world in general believed in special providences and in everyday suspensions and variations in trains of orderly sequence.

Today's greatest thinkers concede to the omnipotence and omnipresence of Law. To consider it anything less than God in

orderly manifestation would dishonor and limit Deity, imply-
ing that God is self-contradictory and lawless.

There is no space, place, condition, individual, or group that
is exempt from Natural Law. The crystal dewdrop, the gentle
breeze, the shimmering wavelet, the fleecy cloud and the re-
splendent sunset are all just as they are by the mandate of
Law. The graceful proportion and peculiar shade of every leaf,
flower, plant, and tree are specified by Law. The rain, the tor-
nado, the earthquake, heat and cold, all scrupulously observe
the Law. The fashioning of the bird's wing and the insect's foot
is regulated by Law. Plagues, pestilences and famines come by
Law. Orders of mammals, birds, fish, and reptiles appear on
the earth, run their course, and disappear according to Law.

But higher than these, the human being thinks, wills, imag-
ines, and develops—physically, mentally, and spiritually—by Law.
Institutions, governments, civilizations, and religions all owe
their histories, peculiar developments, and success or failure
to their relationship with Law. Pain, joy, blessing and all other
kinds of consciousness are ordained by Law. Even signs, wonders, and miracles are within its all-embracing boundaries—
although the keen search of science may yet have failed to discover their footsteps or pathways.

Is, then, this all-comprehensive Law mechanical, merciless,
tyrannical? Are we the helpless victims of a universal system,
every detail of which is unavoidable and inevitable? No, not
victims, but *victors*.

This book teaches the Natural Laws that apply to the Body,
Mind and Soul—laws that humanity has lived largely in ignorance of. Law itself is infinitely intelligent, perfect, and beneficent. However, it requires more than a superficial glance at the
subject to conclude that.

A characteristic of Law is that friction, pain, and penalty result from its violation. Penalty is the shock we feel when we collide with Law. Speaking exactly, Law itself cannot be broken. If we transgress it, the Law remains intact, and we are broken.

This is for the best. If Law could in any degree be bent to conform to our variable wishes or standards, the moral and physical universe would become chaos. Penalty is not calamitous and does not originate from without. Rather, it is inherent, subjective, corrective—and therefore good. Even human statutory penalties for the violation of imperfect legislative codes are only intended as corrective and preventive measures, both for the criminal and society. The vindictive element that formerly manifested itself in punitive stripes and tortures—in the spirit of "an eye for an eye"—has largely passed away except, perhaps, for a lingering remnant in that form known as *capital punishment.*

Pain is penalty, whether physical, mental, or spiritual, and comes from the bruises we receive from avoidable collision with Law. But the Law itself sustains not the least fracture. It continues on its smooth, harmonious course without deflection or interruption. Pain appears to be an armed and vindictive enemy, but it is really a friend in disguise. If we look beneath its mask and recognize and accept it, it takes us by the hand and gently leads us back from the "thorny thicket" through which we were plunging under the command of passion, ignorance, or weakness. Then we can travel the smooth path Law has made for our resistless progress.

Law is our judge and pain is the judgment. *The cure for suffering is the recognition of its friendly mission which makes its judgment accepted and confessed.* If we struggle against penalty and insist that it has been misdirected, or that it descends on us from any outside source, it grows in intensity. Judgment denied enforces its stern demands. If passion, animalism, and selfishness were not warned off and held in check by prospective penalty, how soon the otherwise beautiful human economy would become a wreck.

In our higher nature we find a correspondence of more profound depth and intensity. Pain and remorse—physical and mental—are the severe judgment of sin, materialism, and moral debasement. These monitors rise up and eloquently appeal to us to turn about and come into harmony with Law.

Judgment unheeded and defied at length becomes hell. While the old theological monstrosity of a God-made hell is a myth, we actually create hells of our own. When our natures become disordered and perverted, Law kindly incites a hellish condition to goad us into turning back, so we don't forever drift away from the harmony of God and Law and thus destroy ourselves. Hell is a necessity. Heavenly love and beneficent Law fan its primitive flames—not the anger of a wrathful Deity. If sin did not inevitably carry penalty in its wake, people would keep on sinning forever. The farther the "prodigal sons" move away from God in consciousness, the more intense becomes their self-inflicted penalty until they finally turn their faces back toward the Father's house.

Only when our selfishness and ignorance foolishly antagonize the Law does it seem baneful to our distorted vision. Through dark and superstitious periods in the past, beneficent Law seemed so unfriendly that we interpreted it as an evil personality and cringed in fear of it.

Instead, we may make law our infinitely powerful ally. For example, when we use electricity in accordance with its own laws, it multiplies our physical accomplishments a thousand fold. On the contrary, if we disregard its orderly methods and strive to impose our own rational theories on it, we receive the judgment of penalty. It is the same with the laws that govern our bodies, minds, and souls.

As we render ourselves plastic to Natural Law's healthful persuasion and parallel her lines instead of crossing them, we enlist the potential of the universe in our service. Disregarding it, we kick against the urgings. Yet through Law's cordial cooperation we may accomplish all things. As Emerson said, "Hitch your wagon to a star." God's wise, moral economy provides that we who are made in God's image should use God's methods. Intelligent recognition of this great boon makes us princely in power and God-like in character. No longer being a slave to law, we can, through its instrumentality, not only be free ourselves but also command Divine prerogatives and privileges.

Some might argue, and with great plausibility, that some Natural Laws are hostile to humanity and utterly beyond our control—for instance, those that produce earthquakes, tornadoes, hurricanes, and typhoons, which often seem to sweep humanity out of existence. From a material standpoint, these are evil.

But truth lies deeper. What is their significance, and how do they relate to mankind? Convulsions of Nature are throes, or growing pains, in the progressive development of the physical universe. The phenomena of cataclysms and deluges are but the natural results of great onward sweeps of cosmic evolution. As to how they relate to humanity, they cannot harm us at any point. True, they may blot out our physical expression, but in reality that is no intrinsic part of us.

From the "body" standpoint, material dissolution is the king of evils. But we are not body, and the physical point of view is false. Only by a general degradation is our flesh-consciousness identified with the ego. It is this mistake, and only this, that clothes physical calamities with their terror.

Reasoning from the basis of the *real*, evils can only be evils from their subjective moral quality. A stroke of lightning deprives someone of bodily expression. The *person* is intact. His or her means of material correspondence is removed, but morally that person is no worse. Therefore, no evil has befallen. The change is in the person's relations and environment, not in the person nor in the veritable "I am," the consciousness that forms his or her real being. It is a false and debased sense of life that makes it consist only of physical sensations. Such is animal life; but the human is a "living Soul."

Only when we rise to the standpoint of the *real* can our ordinary, distorted view of that evolutionary "step across," be recognized as the subjective absence of good. Only a thorough materialist can deny the truth of these premises and deductions.

The beneficence of Law is therefore not disproved by any *apparent* hostility on the part of Nature's forces. Plagues and pestilences result from violating Law—or rather from not recognizing the power and utility of *higher laws* with which we can ally ourselves to overcome and banish these conditions.

While Natural Law is never suspended, there are mental and spiritual laws which rule and neutralize the power of those laws that are below. Our divinely invested soul gives us dominion in the subordinate realm. You lift a pebble from the ground, thus overcoming the law of gravitation with the higher law of the human will. But not for an instant is the earth's attraction lessened or suspended.

Spiritual laws occupy the highest rank in beneficence and

potential and, therefore, are primary and causative forces. The intellectual economy is inferior in rank, being expressive and resultant. The physical realm is a still cruder manifestation of the immaterial forces that have their source and play in unseen productive agencies. We speak of the "Laws of Matter," but matter has no laws of its own. It merely expresses the quality and shaping of what is back of, and superior to, itself.

We must discern the fact that we are the sharers and heirs of the Divine Nature, and that with such a heritage we may assert our birthright of authority over the economies around and below us. We learn to govern, mold, and give quality to our own natures as we comprehend and use the forces of the spiritual world from which the innumerable lines of Law radiate and gather their potential.

Whenever our consciousness rises above the selfish animality that darkens the basement of our being and looks out through the spiritual attitude of our nature, we intuitively feel the kindness of established order and know that Law is *good*. Law is not only supremely powerful, but it is ever waiting to serve us.

The human body is but a literal transcript of the mind. Physical inharmonies can be rectified through mental and spiritual lawfulness. But because the process is complex and gradual, the correspondence is not superficially apparent. Every living thing grows into the likeness of its environment. We can invoke the true or the false and surround ourselves with it as if by magic. Through obedience to Law, we are creators and can build subjective worlds. Before long, the objective sphere takes on those qualities.

A study of health is vastly more profitable than a study of disease, because every mental delineation presses toward outward structural expression. Through understanding and applying the Natural Laws that govern the Body, Mind, and Soul, we may consciously and voluntarily cooperate with the Divine in our own evolutionary progress.

FOR MORE INFORMATION

Congratulations on finishing this book!

If its message about enhancing your life through understanding and applying the Natural Laws of the Body, Mind, and Soul strikes you as a worthwhile pursuit, you've joined tens of thousands of other individuals who would agree. Many of them meet regularly across the U.S. and Canada in study groups that are devoted to discussing and analyzing the life-changing message of *Rays of the Dawn*.

If you want to deepen your knowledge and increase your effectiveness through participation in a study group, please contact us for information about the one nearest you. Other materials that you may find helpful in bringing positive change into your life include:

- *Rays of the Dawn Self-Evaluation Booklet*, designed to help you "Zero in on the Laws of Life" to attain health, happiness, success, and peace—as a unit
- *Rays of the Dawn Correlated Course of Study*, a self-paced study guide to assist you in better understanding the Laws of the Body, Mind, and Soul, and applying them positively to everyday life
- *Am I All of That?*, a pictorial version of *Rays of the Dawn*, written for children ages 6-12
- *Total Health Image Through Relaxation*, an audiocassette with a guided relaxation and total health suggestion on Side one, and "Soothing Sounds of Nature" on Side two
- *Inner-Klean Diet: A Six-Day Diet to Remove Toxins from the Body*, an easy-to-read pamphlet
- *Balanced Meals*, a booklet of scientifically combined, easy-to-follow menus

- *Where There Is a Will, There Is a Way: A Biography of Thurman Fleet*, D.C., the inspiring, fascinating, and often poignant story of the author's journey through life, written by his son, George Thurman Fleet, Jr.

If you are really motivated to change your life, you may wish to enroll in a weekend course in Concept-Therapy®, which offers additional, comprehensive instruction in the Laws of Life. Taught nationwide, the course has a complete money back guarantee: *Take the entire course of instruction and if you are not completely satisfied with what you have learned, request a refund from the instructor at the end of the class. The amount paid as tuition will be returned then and there.* The fact that the Concept-Therapy Institute has operated under this broad, inclusive guarantee since the 1930s attests to both the value of the philosophy and the integrity of the organization.

Our best to you as you journey through life!

Call toll-free today: 1-800-531-5628
www.concept-therapy.org

Concept-Therapy Institute
25550 Boerne Stage Road
San Antonio, TX 78255-9565
210-698-2254

The Concept-Therapy Institute, Inc., has been in continuous operation since its inception in 1931. Located since 1949 on a 318-acre campus in suburban San Antonio, TX, the Institute is a state-chartered, not-for-profit, federally tax-exempt educational organization, as defined in Section 501 (c) (3) of the Internal Revenue Code.

ABOUT THE AUTHOR

Dr. Thurman Fleet
(1895-1983)

Born in Blacksburg, Virginia, George Thurman Fleet was founder of the Concept-Therapy Institute in San Antonio, Texas. He had a distinguished, multifaceted career that encompassed first the military, then health care, and later wholistic health education. In each area he demonstrated loyalty, intelligence, an unwavering dedication to ideals, and an abiding desire to understand life and assist humanity in its upward progression.

While serving in the U.S. Army in WWI under the command of Gen. John J. Pershing, Sgt. Fleet went into battle with the 26th Infantry in France. He received a battlefield promotion to the rank of Captain, and was awarded this country's second highest medal, the Distinguished Service Cross. He also received the Silver Star, the Purple Heart, the coveted French Croix de Guerre with Palm, and the French Legion of Honor. For the remainder of his life, Capt. Fleet was an active member of the Legion of Valor, whose membership is limited to those decorated for gallantry with the Medal of Honor, the Distinguished Service Cross, or the Navy Cross.

After surviving horrific wartime experiences and a prolonged recovery from severe injuries, he felt compelled to learn about health and healing, so he entered the chiropractic field.

Nineteen thirty-one was a pivotal year. Not only did Dr. Fleet graduate from the Texas Chiropractic College, but he immediately began applying his knowledge with scores of patients and soon had a successful private practice in San Antonio.

That December, a "peak experience" in consciousness inspired Dr. Fleet to uncover the fundamental principles of the human personality and their relationship to the natural laws of life. He did this by researching more than 30,000 published sources. From this massive effort he developed a comprehensive, correlated approach to understanding life and

healing, a philosophy he named Concept-Therapy®—*working/
healing with ideas*. One singular document, *Rays of the Dawn*,
emerged initially as a series of pamphlets to help his patients
understand their role in creating health. In 1948, Dr. Fleet
copyrighted and published the material in book form.

The idea for founding the Concept-Therapy Institute as a
nonprofit, educational organization also took root in 1931. By
1944, Dr. Fleet was teaching the Concept-Therapy philosophy
to members of the various healing professions. In the early
1950s, classes were opened to laypersons, and the organization
grew into a wholistic health education institution.

Dr. Fleet served as President of the Concept-Therapy Institute
until 1960, when he became advisor to the Board of Control, a
position he held until his death in 1983. He was interred with
full military honors in the Ft. Sam Houston National Cemetery,
San Antonio, Texas.